JAMAICA

IAN SANGSTER

A Benn Holiday Guide

ERNEST BENN LIMITED / LONDON & TONBRIDGE

First published 1973
by Ernest Benn Limited
Sovereign Way, Tonbridge, Kent, &
25 New Street Square, London, EC4A 3JA

Distributed in Canada by
The General Publishing Company Limited, Toronto
Typeset by Transeuroset, Potters Bar, England
Printed in Italy by
Il Resto del Carlino, Bologna
ISBN 0 510-02970-1
0510-02971-X (Paperback)

FOR FIONA AND MORAG

Overleaf: Dawn in Portland

INTRODUCTION

Jamaica must contain a greater variety of landscape and people in its 4 411 square miles than any other island or country of comparable size. The terrain varies from towering mountains to palm fringed white beaches; from lush meadows to near jungle. Pine trees grow in the Blue Mountains, where one needs a sweater in the evenings, while crocodiles inhabit steamy mangrove swamps on the south coast. Sugar cane, bananas, coconut, citrus and coffee are the main crops but the island's climate and topography are so varied that almost anything can be grown in some part of it. The population is predominantly Negro, descendants of the original slaves, but most other races and ethnic groups are represented, as well as most possible racial mixtures. The result is a racial kaleidoscope of great interest and beauty, and relationships between races are a lesson to some larger, richer and allegedly more educated countries, as no colour bar exists and interracial conflict is virtually unknown.

To the visitor Jamaica offers a bewildering variety of experiences; from climbing in the Blue Mountains to exploring the fascinating limestone caves under many parts of the island; from water-skiing to skin-diving around the beautiful coral reefs; from ruined reminders of the turbulent past to ultra-modern hotels and clubs. With a temperature difference of less than six degrees fahrenheit between summer and what Jamaicans regard as winter (average in July is 80°, in January 75°) the sea is always pleasantly warm. (Paradoxically, few Jamaicans can swim.)

Tourism is growing, with over half a million visitors in 1972. Most come from North America. They are catered for mainly in north coast resorts such as Montego Bay and Ocho Rios, which areas are consequently more expensive and less Jamaican than any other part of the island.

Jamaica has two faces, of which the casual visitor normally sees only one, getting as he does a quick impression of the beauty and history of the country, and of the informality which characterises Jamaican society. The less beautiful face, caused by economic difficulties and the poverty of most of its inhabitants, is not so obvious.

Almost one third of Jamaica's 1 900 000 people live in and around the capital, Kingston, and more people from the rural areas are being attracted daily, seeking work. This introduces a less 'island in the sun' aspect of Jamaica, which is experiencing all the challenges and frustrations of a developing country. The basic problem is that most food and consumer goods are imported, as are oil, steel, motor vehicles and the majority of manufactured goods. Bauxite and the above mentioned crops are exported, but each year sees a large trade gap and the task of closing it brings Jamaica up against the problem of most small countries, – that of competing with the big producers – be they producing sugar or automobiles. A population which increases yearly, despite a vigorous birth control programme, adds to the difficulties. In common with most countries, the cost of living is rising steadily. Some of the prices given in this guide will thus be out of date by the time you are reading this, but they will serve to give a guide to the relative and general costs. The dollar quoted is, in all cases, the Jamaican dollar.

This, then is Jamaica, a country of great beauty and natural riches, whose people nevertheless still leave in their thousands for harsher climates. It is an island which enchants and saddens simultaneously, and the many facets and moods of country and people present both an enigma and a delight to the sensitive visitor.

USEFUL BOOKS

Birds of the West Indies by James Bond (Collins, Glasgow). *Introduction to the Birds of Jamaica* by Lady Taylor (Institute of Jamaica, Kingston). *Birds and Flowers of Jamaica* by Margaret K. Rhodes (Novelty Trading Co., Ltd., Kingston). *Bird Watching in Jamaica* by May Jeffrey-Smith (Bolivar, Kingston). *The Blue Mahoe and other Bush* by C. Dennis Adams (Sangster, Kingston). *Tropical Trees (found in the Caribbean etc.)* by Dorothy and Bob Hargreaves also *Tropical Blossoms of the Caribbean* by Dorothy and Bob Hargreaves (both by Hargreaves, Hawaii). *The Botanic Gardens of Jamaica* by Alan Eyre (André Deutsch, London). *History of Jamaica* by Clinton V. Black (Collins, Glasgow). *Lady Nugent's Journal* (ed. Philip Wright) (Institute of Jamaica, Kingston).

Acknowledgements

Thanks are due to the following for the use of their photographs on the pages noted:

Jamaican Tourist Board for: 9, 16, 21, 22, 23, 27, 80 & 81; David Lee for: 18; Ingolf Duphorn for: 29; Lothar Böhm for: 10; 30; James Chong for: 48; The remainder are by the author.

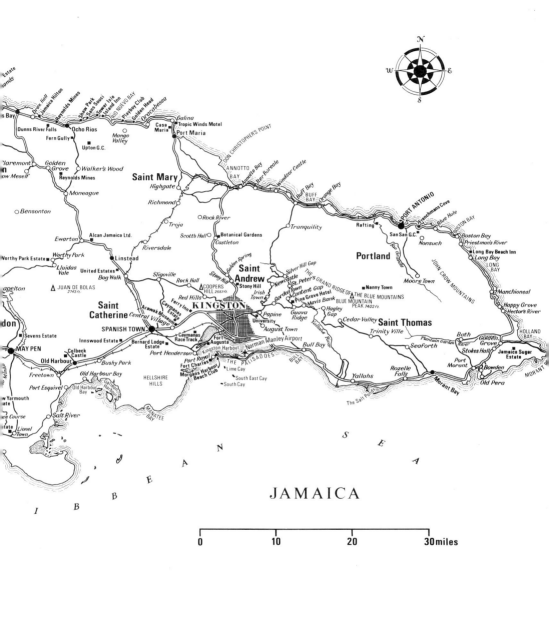

JAMAICA

0   10   20   30 miles

PLACE

Geography. Between Florida and the mainland of South America stretches a fascinating chain of large and small islands, the Greater and the Lesser Antilles. Jamaica belongs to the former, along with Cuba (90 miles to the north), Haiti (100 miles east), the Dominican Republic, and Puerto Rico. The chain encloses the Caribbean sea, terminating 1 000 miles from Jamaica in Trinidad, off the coast of Venezuela. Jamaica is roughly 2 000 miles from New York and Toronto, 5 000 miles from London, 600 miles from Miami, and 500 from the Panama Canal. The island, 146 miles long and 51 miles across at its broadest point, has a shape which has, with some justification, been likened to a swimming turtle, and displays within its small area a bewildering range of scenery. The eastern end is dominated by the great ridge of the Blue Mountains, running west to south-east, with many spurs to north and south. Rising from the sea to over 7 000 ft. in less than 10 miles, it has few rivals in the world for dramatic beauty. Valleys have been cut by cascading rivers such as the Yallahs and Hope Rivers which drain the south side of the ridge, and the Rio Grande and Buff Bay Rivers on the north side. Many minor ranges of mountains and hilly uplands occupy the centre of the island and almost half the total area is over 1 000 ft. above sea level. The volcanic rocks of the Blue Mountains are the oldest part of Jamaica, dating from the Cretaceous period (i.e. over 100 million years old). Most of the younger hills and plateaus are limestone, the most dramatic example being the Cockpit country to the south of Falmouth, where rainfall has moulded the limestone landscape into a tortured system of conical hills and sink holes (likened to cockpits, thus the name), looking for all the world like some vast green egg box. The region, covering over 200 square miles, can only be penetrated on foot, and that with difficulty. (It is thus a favoured haven for growing *ganja*, as marijuana is locally known). As in all limestone country there are numerous underground rivers, with the resulting formation of many large caves, some of which can be penetrated for miles, (see *spelunking*, page 18).

Jamaica's coastline is very varied. The east coast, which takes a steady pounding from seas driven by the prevailing north-east trade wind, is rugged and indented by many small bays and coves such as Boston Bay and Blue Hole. The north coast has calm seas and white sand beaches, attributes which reach their peak at Negril on the south-west coast, which has 7 miles of beautiful, white, palm fringed beach, protected by a magnificent reef, as are many of the north coast beaches. The south coast in St Catherine, Clarendon, St Elizabeth and Westmorland has large areas of coastal plain, interspersed with cliffs such as the 1 500 ft.high Lover's Leap, in St Elizabeth. Around Black River the low lying coastal plain saturates under the impact of four rivers to form the Great Morass, where crocodiles are found, shrimps abound, and oysters grow on trees (literally, on the submerged portions of mangrove trees).

Climate. This should more accurately be in the plural, as the varied topography of the island causes a wide variety of climatic conditions. The closeness of all parts of the island to the Caribbean Sea has a moderating influence on the temperature, making the climate maritime-tropical, influenced by the north-east trade wind. The Blue Mountains affect both temperature and rainfall markedly, and cause wide variations in each with change in location. The average temperature on the coast is 80°F (27°C) while at Newcastle in the Blue Mountains (4 000 ft.) it is only 67°F (19°C). There are two wet seasons, the first in May–June and the second (wetter) one in September–October, this being part of the August-September-October hurricane season. Since 1886 Jamaica has been hit by nineteen hurricanes, the last being in 1944, and has felt the effects of ninety eight which passed within 150 miles of the island.

The most pleasant season for the normal run of human beings is winter, from November to April, with the coolest and driest period being January to March.

On the coast, the temperature is subject to the moderating influence of coastal winds caused by thermal differences between land and sea. Early in the day, the breeze blows from the sea, reviving those unfortunate enough to have to work in the heat, and named gratefully the

'Doctor Wind'. Later in the afternoon a second breeze blows from the land, which, in conjunction with the evening temperature drop, could cause a chill in those still hot and sweating from the afternoon's toil. This is respectfully referred to as the 'Undertaker Wind'.

Government. Jamaica is a constitutional monarchy under the British Crown, and is a member of the British Commonwealth. The Queen is represented by the Governor General (known locally as the 'gee-gee'). The island was a Crown Colony from the Morant Bay Rebellion of 1865 (see page 62), until 1938 when the cousins Norman Manley and Alexander Bustamante (affectionately known as 'Busta', and whose original name was Clarke) catalysed labour-political movements which were instrumental in obtaining self-government. The cousins were poles apart in character, and this difference was reflected in the political parties they founded. Bustamante, at various times policeman in Cuba, tramway inspector in Panama, dietician in New York and money-lender in Jamaica, relied for his success on personal charisma and understanding of the masses. In 1938 he founded a trade union called, characteristically, after himself and followed this by founding the *Jamaica Labour Party (JLP)* in 1943. Manley, by contrast, was an intellectual, educated at Oxford, and was an eminent Queen's Counsel when he formed the *People's National Party (PNP)* in 1938. The PNP is traditionally more socialistic than the JLP, the difference parallelling that between the British Labour and Conservative parties, and is affiliated to Jamaica's other trade union, the National Workers' Union. During the war years Bustamante was imprisoned for obstructing the war effort, but immediately after the British granted Jamaica a new constitution and universal adult sufferage. In 1962, Bustamante was largely responsible for torpedoing the ill-fated West Indies Federation by successfully campaigning for Jamaica's secession (a referendum showed a 35 000 majority in favour of Jamaican withdrawal), and the country became independent from Britain in the same year. The present Government, elected in 1972, is PNP under the Prime Ministership of Michael Manley, the son of Norman. Both Sir Alexander Bustamante and the late Norman Manley have been elevated to the status of national heroes and along with Marcus Garvey, and with Paul Bogle and William Gordon of Morant Bay Rebellion fame, their faces grace Jamaica's banknotes.

For administrative purposes the island is divided into fourteen parishes, which, with the exception of Kingston and St Andrew which has a mayor and corporation, are run by parochial boards.

Flora. Were Columbus able to return to Jamaica today, he might think he had taken a wrong turn somewhere, such is the change in the island's vegetation since he first landed in 1494. Due to the great variation of climate and topography, most plant species can grow in some part of the island and the hundreds of imported plants which have become established have resulted in a spectrum of types and colours equalled by few other countries. Of the pre-1494 Jamaican trees, the most prominent are:

Mahoe, *Hibiscus elatus*, Jamaica's national tree, the Blue Mahoe, so called on account of the attractive blue or blue-green streaks in the grain of the wood, used locally for furniture and building. The trees can grow to over 60 ft. and produce large flowers which change gradually from yellow to red before falling. The name Mahoe is of Carib Indian origin.

Pimento, *Pimenta dioica*, also called Jamaica Pepper, or Allspice, is the only indigenous plant to become a major export crop (Jamaica is the world's largest producer). The tree bears small green berries which, when dried, resemble black peppers. Here the resemblance ends, as pimento is a very aromatic spice, whose flavour and scent resemble a blend of cloves, cinnamon and nutmeg. The leaves are a valuable source of pimento oil.

Ceiba, *Ceiba pentandra*, or Silk Cotton, grows to great size and age, and can be identified by the buttress-like roots radiating out from the grey trunk. Ceiba has been used by fishermen since Arawak times to make dugout canoes.

Papaya, *Carica jamaicensis*, also known as Pawpaw, this weird little plant has a hollow trunk bearing a few large, hand-shaped leaves which have the ability to render tough meat tender. The mature pawpaw fruit resembles a cross between mango and melon and can be eaten either as desert or made into a rather thick but pleasant nectar. The immature fruit is used as a vegetable.

Imported trees of economic importance include:

Banana, *Musa sapientum*, introduced around 1520 by the Spaniards. The large hanging purple flower sheds its petals as the stem grows, leaving residual stubs which grow into 'hands' of bananas. A bunch consists of several hands. A related fruit is the larger and less sweet plantain.

Coconut, *Cocos nucifera*, was also introduced by the Spaniards. The predominant type was formerly the graceful tall palm which, sadly, has been killed off in recent years by Lethal Yellowing Disease, and is being replaced by the Malayan Dwarf species which is more resistant but which lacks the wild beauty of the tall variety. The milk from young coconuts is a popular and very refreshing drink on a hot day.

Breadfruit, *Artocarpus incisa*, was brought to Jamaica in 1793 by Captain William Bligh (of Mutiny fame, the *Bounty* was carrying breadfruit seedlings from Tahiti to the West Indies at the time) and is now a staple part of the Jamaican diet. The large round green fruit can be either boiled or roasted.

Ackee, *Blighia sapida*, is the national fruit of Jamaica. The tree's bright green shiny leaves form a background to masses of red fruit, which open when ripe to reveal three large black seeds set in yellow lobes which can be cooked and eaten. The first seeds were brought from West Africa in a slave ship (the name ackee is of African origin) and soon became established all over the island. Captain Bligh took samples of 'new' Jamaican plants including ackee back to Kew Gardens in London, and was rewarded by having the genus named after him. Bligh also introduced the **Otaheite Apple** (Otaheite is the old name for Tahiti), a maroon fruit, white inside, growing on a tall cone-shaped tree from flowers which resemble little cerise shaving brushes.

Citrus. Orange trees were introduced to the Caribbean from the Canary Islands by Columbus in 1494, and now grow in most parts of Jamaica. Other citrus which grow well in Jamaica are grapefruit, lime, tangerine, and the **ortanique**, developed here by crossing orange with tangerine. The name is a fusion of **or**ange, **tan**gerine and un**ique**.

Mango, *Mangifera indica*, introduced by Admiral Rodney; mangoes are a vital item in the diet of poorer Jamaicans.

Jamaica's profusion of flowering shrubs, trees and cacti range from the transient white loveliness of Night Flowering Cereus, *Hylocereus triangularis*, lasting for only one night, to the bold red leaves of Poinsettia, which flowers over the Christmas period. Among common shrubs are the various species of bouganvillia, hibiscus, jasmine, and begonia. Flowering trees include:

Poinsiana, *Poinsiana regia*, whose spectacular red or orange outburst gives the tree its other name of 'Flamboyant'.

Golden Shower, *Cassia Fistula*, which erupts into an unfortunately short-lived yellow exuberance, covering the ground under it in a golden carpet.

Tulip Tree, *Spathodia campanulata* which is a memorable sight when heavy with its large red upright flowers.

Lignum Vitae, *Guaiacum officinale*, producing the small blue national flower of Jamaica. It is an indigenous hardwood.

Jamaica also has over 200 species of native orchid.

Fauna. Jamaica has no large wild animals apart from an ever-decreasing number of crocodiles (called alligators in Jamaica), which inhabit the swamps along the south coast, and have been mercilessly hunted for their skins and for sport. Some wild boars, descendants of the pigs set free by the Spaniards, are still found in parts of the island, but these apart the largest mammal is the coney, or *Jamaica Huita*, a rodent about the size of a rabbit, now restricted to the more remote areas, and rarely seen because of its nocturnal habits. Seen quite frequently, however, is

Colourful roadside markets contribute to the visitor's interest

the **mongoose**, introduced from India during the last century to control rats in the cane fields, and now quite a pest itself, preying on chickens, birds and eggs. Two other items on its menu, the common lizards and the not so common snakes, are both non-poisonous and harmless, although croaker lizards make an alarming noise out of all proportion to their size, a capacity they share with two of Jamaica's fifteen species of **frogs**, the *whistling and snoring tree frogs*. Twenty-two species of bats (called ratbats to distinguish them from large moths, which are also called bats) are to be found, and no batist should miss a chance of seeing them en masse in one of the island's many caves. Jamaica has more than 6 000 insect species, with mosquitos (no malaria carriers) and sandflies normally being the only aggressive ones. Black Widow spiders occur, as do scorpions, but both are rarely seen, whereas harmless fireflies, called *peenie wallies* or *blinkies*, can be seen most evenings.

Of some 250 **bird** species found in Jamaica twenty-four are peculiar to the island:

Doctor Bird or Swallow Tail Humming Bird, *Trochilus polytmus*, the national bird of Jamaica. Both male and female have beautiful irridescent green plumage and red beaks, and the male bird has a long two-feather tail, the similarity of which to the tail coat formerly worn by medical practitioners is said to have given the bird its popular name.

Vervain (or Bee) Humming Bird, *Mellisuga minima*, little over two inches long and smallest of the island's birds.

Turkey Vulture, *Cathartes aura,* largest of the island's birds, and commonly known as 'John Crow'. This great black bird, with its unmistakable bare red head, is ungainly on the ground, but marvellously graceful in flight.

Tody or Robin Redbreast, *Todus todus*, is a remarkable bird with a brilliant emerald-green head and back, crimson chest, orange beak and yellow underparts. It lives in a burrow in the earth.

9

Aqualung diving off reef buttresses

Sub Aqua. Jamaica possesses, off its north coast, one of the finest reefs in the world, composed of more than fifty coral types together with a wide variety of beautiful sponges and seaweeds. It is easily accessible from the beach, and can best be experienced by scuba diving with an air supply, but failing this it can be seen by swimming with mask and snorkel or even from the security of a glass-bottomed boat. Swarms of multicoloured small fish inhabit the reef but the larger species prefer deeper water, although sharks, barracuda (which looks rather like a pike) and stingrays can occasionally be seen inside the reef. There are few instances on record of bathers being attacked by sharks or barracuda in Jamaican waters and the most common cause of underwater injuries are sea urchins (called sea eggs) whose long black spines can penetrate even rubber flippers, causing a painful wound, as they break off and are extremely difficult to remove. Edible fish and crustaceans found off the island's coasts include snapper, mullet, kingfish, crab, shrimps and spiny lobster. Turtles are occasionally seen around the reef and can move surprisingly quickly and gracefully.

Scuba diving requires equipment and organisation, available in Kingston at the Jamaica Sub Aqua Club (Altamont Crescent, near Sheraton Hotel) and from Scuba Jamaica at Montego Bay (beside Palm Beach Hotel) and at Negril (Sundowner Hotel) who supply instruction, gear, boat, and guide. When diving or snorkelling, you should pick up some of the many attractive sea shells found in Jamaican waters, such as the beautiful Queen Conch, a shell whose inhabitant thoughtfully makes a delicious soup. Spear fishing, on account of the closeness of hunter and hunted, is a more energetic and exciting sport than fishing with rod, net or dynamite. Spear guns are available from the above agencies.

Industry and Agriculture. After centuries of being an almost completely agricultural economy, paying for its industrial imports with agricultural exports, Jamaica has, in the last decade, begun to diversify its economy by expanding the industrial sector. The fillip to this process has been given by exploitation of the island's deposits of **bauxite** (the ore from which aluminium is

10

made). Since Spanish times, metals have been mined intermittently in Jamaica, especially copper, the mining of which since 1598 is commemorated in the name of Rio Cobre (Copper River). The only metal now produced is aluminium, and Jamaica is the world's largest producer of bauxite. North American firms such as Kaiser, Reynolds and Alcan open-cast mine the red earth (bauxite is a mixture of white alumina and red iron oxides) which covers over a quarter of the island's surface, and ship it or the refined alumina to plants mainly in U.S.A., Canada or Norway, where it is reduced to aluminium. These exports earn Jamaica around $170 million each year.

Gypsum is the main non-metallic mineral produced, annual production being in the region of 200 000 tons. Most of this goes to U.S.A., but around 20 000 tons are consumed by Kingston's neolithic cement works. No oil or natural gas occurs in Jamaica, and imported crude oil is refined in Kingston.

Many smaller industries exist, such as light engineering, brewing, tyre manufacture, a variety of assembly, or in local terms 'screwdriver' industries, and an expanding food processing industry.

Jamaica's history is inextricably entwined with that of **sugar** and in agriculture, sugar cane production and processing is still the biggest revenue earner and employer of labour, roughly one third of cultivated land producing sugar cane. The distribution of soil types and climatic conditions suitable for cane growing is very wide, and it occurs in all fourteen parishes.

The present total of fifteen sugar factories will certainly shrink as the efficiencies of large-scale operation squeeze the smaller factories out, and production is concentrated in the most suitable areas. Cane is hand cut by a large force of machete-swinging cane cutters, and taken by truck or trailer (on the hill farms initially by donkey) to the factory. Here huge rollers crush out the juice, which, after being clarified and evaporated down to a syrup, is run into vacuum pans and crystallisers. Here the brown sugar crystallises out and is removed, leaving behind molasses. This, on being fermented and distilled, yields the famous **Jamaican Rums**, production of which exceeds 3 million proof gallons per year. Sugar, rum and molasses exports earn Jamaica over $50 million each year. Other important agricultural export crops, with their approximate export values, are bananas ($12 million), citrus ($5 million), pimento ($3 million), coffee ($2 million), cocoa ($1.5 million).

Great Houses and Ruins. Little of Jamaica's Spanish building survives apart from the ruins excavated at the old capital, Sevilla Nueva. From the early English Period, commencing 1655, only a few buildings, albeit an impressive few, remain. These include **Stokes Hall**, (circa 1710) in St Thomas, a massive stone fortified house with two-storied towers at each corner of its 50 ft. by 30 ft. centre. Loopholes in the walls testify to the determination of its defenders to resist whatever was to be resisted. **Fort Charles** at Port Royal survived the 1692 earthquake and is the sole remainder of the pirate capital. **Halse Hall**, 3 miles south of May Pen, was built by Major Thomas Halse, who came to Jamaica with Penn and Venables, and is buried (1702) in the adjacent burial ground. The house, now restored, has an interesting old Jamaican sanitary feature. In front, in a position of prominence, is a small square building with a 'candle-snuffer' roof. This is a seventeenth century 'three holer' communal privy, whose single-plank three-seater in fact makes no concessions to privacy at all! **Seville Great House** (circa 1745), near St Ann's Bay, has been continuously occupied and has recently been restored.

Colbeck Castle, north of Old Harbour, is the largest and most fascinating of all Jamaica's ruins. It is uncertain when it was built, or by whom, or for what, or indeed, if it was ever lived in! Its roofless 100 ft. by 90 ft. walls and great three-storied square towers now shelter bats and lizards, and those who could dispel its mysteries are centuries dead. Most early plantation houses appear, from contemporary accounts, to have been simple, makeshift affairs, and often the sugar factory buildings were much more solid and attractive than the planter's house. This is demonstrated by such magnificient sugar ruins as **Kenilworth** in Hanover, **Orange Valley**, **Kent** and **Good Hope**, near Falmouth, and the **University Chapel**, itself once a sugar

The University Chapel UWI

factory building. Many of the sugar mills were driven by water, and impressive remnants of some of the massive **aqueducts** built to carry it can be seen at Mona, Hope, Worthy Park and Bushy Park. An alternative source of power was wind, and all over the island can be seen remnants of sugar windmills which are witnesses, along with the factory ruins and aqueducts, to the passing of the 750 sugar factories which operated in Jamaica during sugar's eighteenth-century boom years. During the eighteenth century, some splendid plantation Great Houses were built, usually on a high point on the property, commanding views in all directions. These included **Rose Hall**, one of the largest and most beautiful of Jamaican houses, built around 1760 at a cost of £30,000 – a vast sum then. A three-storey block with curved side wings, it fell into disuse in 1827 and remained neglected until its recent restoration by an American businessman.

Many other fine houses were built during this period, including *Cinnamon Hill* near Rose Hall, *Good Hope* and **Green Park**, near Falmouth, and **Marlborough** near Mandeville. Most houses are of fundamentally Georgian type, modified to suit tropical conditions, and thus create a distinct Jamaican vernacular style with such characteristic features as wooden shingled multiple roofs to reduce wind resistance; a stone ground level with a central arched passage leading from the double front staircase under the house, which was usually wooden; wide shady verandas, and louvered windows to allow the breeze to pass through the house. Decoration was restrained, and the beauty of local hardwoods complemented the simplicity of design. Characteristic exterior embellishments which have developed from the Jamaican vernacular are decorative and often intricate fretwork on eaves and barge-boards, and ornately wrought iron-work, a good example of which is **De Montevin Lodge** in Port Antonio.

PEOPLE

Origins. Jamaica is a multiracial society, the majority of whose citizens are black. The 'missing link' in Jamaica's population is the **Arawak**, the original Indian people of the island, but with this exception, all successive waves of immigrants have contributed to the fascinating amalgam of present-day society.

A relic of the **Spanish** occupation is a substantial colony of **Jewish** families, whose forebears came to Jamaica after the expulsion of Jews from Spain in 1492. They are commemorated by names such as *daCosta, Levy, deLeon, Lopez, deSouza, Lascelles* and *deMercado*.

The **British**, although settled in Jamaica since 1655 have, since the rise of the sugar industry and the subsequent importation of slaves, always constituted a small, albeit dominant, sector of the community. Over the years they were reinforced by European settlers from other areas, such as the many American loyalists who settled in Jamaica in the 1780's after the War of Independence, and the French refugees from neighbouring Haiti who came after the successful slave revolt there in 1793. The last significant influx occurred immediately after emancipation in 1834, when the Government encouraged the importation of European settlers by offering a bounty of £15 for each. One man who found this offer attractive was a **German**, Dr. Wilhelm Lemonius, an ex-Officer in the Prussian army latterly practising medicine in Jamaica. Returning to Germany in 1834, he persuaded over a thousand peasants and artisans from the Weser region of northern Germany to sail for Jamaica's tropical paradise and the promise of free land for all. He omitted to mention, however, that yellow fever and malaria were rife in Jamaica. Within a year, half of the immigrants had died, and of the remainder, many settled in the barren hills around Seaford Town in Westmorland, where, until the present day, they form an in-bred, blonde, blue-eyed community of several hundred, with names such as *Kamicka, Hacker, Eldermeier, Sanftleben* and *Wedermeier*.

The **black majority** of Jamaicans are descendants of the slaves imported (over six hundred thousand of them during the eighteenth century) by the British. They came mainly from the West Coast of Africa and represented many tribes and cultures. On being sold, members of tribes and indeed of families were separated by the planters wherever possible, so that the present-day black Jamaicans are a fusion of all the contributing groups. Yet in spite of attempts to fragment tribes, there must have been an understandable tendency for members of the same tribe to associate with each other with consequent intra-tribal breeding. As a possible result of this, black Jamaicans constitute a population of distinct physical types. Emerging from the colonial era, with its racial attitudes still under the shadow of slavery, they have developed in recent years a new pride in their colour and in their African heritage. A manifestation of this is the rejection by younger Jamaicans of simulated European fashion in dress, hairstyle, art and music, and a return to African roots and rhythms for inspiration. The movement, demonstrated by the *Afro* hairstyles and dress of the young and heard in the heavy, characteristic beat of local dance music such as *Reggae* and *Ska*, finds its most extreme expression in the 'back to Africa' movement of the Rastafarian sect

Brother West of the Rastafarians   *A trustful street vendor*

The white planters who, with few exceptions were not the most enlightened or liberal of men, nevertheless had no objections to taking female slaves as mistresses. The 'coloured' progeny of these relationships were free (but not as free as whites) and came to form an important sector of Jamaican society, the **'free coloureds'**. During slavery, great attention was paid to the amount of negro blood possessed, and a complex colour scale evolved, e.g. *mulatto* – offspring of white and negro, *quadroon* – offspring of white and mulatto, *octoroon* – offspring of white and quadroon, etc., etc. Nowadays the term *brown* or *red* is used to cover all such racial mixtures. The brown-skinned 15% of the Jamaican population now constitute the majority of the middle class and are responsible for most of the administration. They are also, perhaps, the only true Jamaican sector of the community, since the whites tend to look to Britain or North America for inspiration and the blacks to Africa. The browns, being neither black nor white have to look to Jamaica. After Emancipation most of the ex-slaves had no desire to work further in sugar, turning instead to small holdings in the hills. To fill their places, two groups of indentured labourers were brought in; thirty-six thousand East Indians and several thousand **Chinese**. Indentures were for five years in return for a free passage. One third of the East Indians (called 'coolies' in Jamaica) but hardly any of the Chinese elected to return home. Also whereas the East Indians have largely stayed in the sugar industry, the Chinese soon forsook labouring to make the retail business, especially of foods, almost their own. They are now the island's shopkeepers and one of the wealthiest sections of society. The last small group of immigrants were the **Syrians** (also called Lebanese) who have demonstrated an aptitude for business equal to that of the Jews and Chinese.

Present Day. Jamaica is a country with problems, and the wonder is not that this is so, but rather that the problems are not greater.

Examine the situation: a country 150 miles long, largely mountainous, with one of the highest population densities in the world and the majority of its people the descendants of slaves freed just over 100 years ago. These slaves, removed from their own society and culture, forced into bondage in a strange land, then set free to fend unassisted for themselves, have achieved a miracle of adjustment and progress in developing so far in so short a time. However, effects of slavery persist, and one of the most enduring is the propensity of many male Jamaicans to shirk family responsibilities. This has resulted in a loose family structure, with a high level (over 70%) of illegitimate births and a lack of paternal responsibility for such offspring. Thus, many if not most, male children are raised by their mother and/or grandmother (quote 'to grow wid de granny'). Lacking male authority, they tend to develop largely feminine attitudes and logic, responding more to affection and request than to discipline and command, and being upset when the same plethora of excuses which satisfied granny are not accepted by employers.

Service industries are poor in Jamaica, perhaps because service is equated with servility, and many shop-keepers, waiters and post-office assistants, etc. do not trouble to disguise their resentment of their task. Advertisers assure Jamaicans that life is not complete without modern amenities which most of them cannot afford, and some, frustrated, turn to crime to obtain them. Robberies have increased sharply and it is no longer safe to walk alone on the streets of Kingston at night, or to venture into some of the rougher areas of the capital.

Women have played a dominant role in Jamaican society since slavery, when through them was effected the fusion of Europe and Africa which produced the brown 'third force' whose energy as free men did so much to direct the island's history. The matriarchal system has invested Jamaican women with the power to mould the national psyche, but only at the cost of having a disproportionate share of the running of society fall on to their shoulders. They bear and rear the family, run the home and are to be found in all sectors of industry, education, medicine and commerce. However Jamaica solves its problems, its progress will owe much to its women-folk.

14

Friendly traffic policeman   *Old man with his donkey*

Religion. The first **Christian** Church in Jamaica was Roman Catholic, founded by the Spaniards at Sevilla Nueva (now St Ann's Bay) in 1525. Catholicism was banned when the Protestant English captured Jamaica in 1655, and remained so until 1792. The Anglican church supported the social status quo and did nothing to alleviate the lot of the slaves, who found their champions among the various non-conformist churches which began to send preachers to the island in the mid-eighteenth century. After Emancipation in 1838, the Anglican Church continued to be the established church and as such was supported by the general taxes paid by non-Anglicans. This lasted until its dis-establishment in 1865, when the island became a Crown Colony after the Morant Bay revolt.

Cults. Jamaica has some indigenous cults which are fusions of Christianity with West African religion and superstition. They can be grouped together under the title **Pocomania** (attributed to the Spanish 'a little madness' but probably more correctly Pukumina from the African Kumina cult practised in the parish of St Thomas), and have in common that the worshipper, in a self-induced state of trance, believes himself possessed by some spirit which can cure him of illness, make him sing, dance, prophesy, etc. Pocomanians hold that people have a soul which ascends (or descends) to the next life, and also a ghost (*duppy*) which remains behind after death. Another sect, part religious/racist/political, are the Rastafarians, whose members are easily recognisable by their long matted hair and beards. The sect's beliefs have their roots in the Bible and in the Black Nationalism of Marcus Garvey (1885–1940, a Jamaican, the first to preach 'black power' in the U.S.A.). The Rastafarian motto is 'Peace and Love', and the sincere *Rasta* is a peaceful associate of a community to which he does not in his opinion belong. On various tenuous biblical grounds, Rastafarians neither shave nor cut their hair and many grow and smoke ganja (marijuana).

A direct import from Africa is the practice of **Obeah** or black magic, the modern 'obeah man' being a descendant of the African witch doctor. Most communities possess at least one 'four-eyed' man or woman whose advice and spells can be bought to counter illness, ill fortune

15

John Canoe Dancers (Rodney Memorial, Spanish Town)

or the spells of a rival. For example, if unemployment threatens, 'Keep Job Oil' can be bought for application to self, workplace or employer, while 'Oil of Love' will secure the affections of the fickle. The practice of obeah is proscribed by law.

Family. With over 70% of all children illegitimate, the Jamaican family is a larger and more flexible association than the tightly knit unit normal in Europe and those parts of the world which have inherited European conventions. These children fall into two main classes, the first being children of unmarried parents living together in a permanent union. This is the so-called *common-law marriage* and one may ask why a couple living together like this do not legalize their union. Among contributing deterrents are first the fact that a wedding in this society is an elaborate and expensive affair, perhaps as a visible proof to the world that the couple really are married, and second a fear that marriage leads to being taken for granted by one's partner. A second group of children have unknown or unobtainable fathers and are brought up by their mothers or by a family complex in which the grandmother looms large. The size of this group accounts for the matriarchial nature of Jamaican society.

These remarks allude to the large Jamaican lower class rather than to the middle class. In the lower income levels, an unmarried girl of over twenty years who has not had at least one child is unusual. This indifference to marriage probably has its roots in the days of slavery when the slave owners, for a variety of selfish reasons, forbade or discouraged their possessions from marrying.

Let it be said that these loose (by European standards) family ties appear to have no adverse effect on either the behaviour or the happiness of Jamaican children.

Education. Jamaica's future development depends largely on how well the population can be taught the complex skills necessary to run modern society. The educational system, with the university as its crown, has its grass roots in small urban and rural schools all over the island, where school attendance is, in theory, compulsory. Education ranges through Infant School, Primary School, Secondary School and Technical College or University. The range of school

16

types runs from expensive boarding schools such as Munro, Decarteret and Hampton, based on English public schools, to village schools where underpaid teachers try to cope with several classes in a single room. With a significant percentage of the adult population effectively illiterate the government launched, in 1972, a national programme of voluntary tuition aimed at 100% adult literacy. Technical education is given at a number of regional centres; agricultural training at the Jamaica School of Agriculture; the Jamaica School of Art, in Kingston, produces a small number of painters, sculptors and potters each year.

Music and Dance. After 1962 Jamaican popular music underwent a significant change. Up till then, it had followed American and British fashions, with some imitation of calypso, which is a Trinidadian art form. Hardly any truly Jamaican music reached the media. Then, suddenly, a dance form which was derived from indigenous cult and folk rhythms and movements swept the country. This was **Ska**, whose insistent beat and arm-swinging dance influenced popular music far from Jamaica. The songs expressed a form of social protest, and sympathy for the angry young men or 'rudies' who were turning to lawlessness, and it certainly helped to stimulate a subsequent crime wave. Ska developed through **Rock Steady** to **Reggae**, with both music and dance becoming more subtle and refined. No public dance halls exist, and dancing is done at house parties (called *jump-ups*). Jamaican music is a fusion of European (mainly British) melodic forms and African rhythms. It includes many sub-types, and a variety of instruments, foremost among which are the drums, which include kumina, tambo, bongo, brukins, congo and bass drums, some beaten with sticks, some with the hands. Other instruments commonly used are fiddle, guitar, banjo, fife, and rhumba box, a series of strings strung over a rectangular sounding box.

This rich heritage finds expression in the performances of such groups as **The Jamaica National Dance Theatre**, and the **Jamaica Folk Singers**, who have incorporated the spontaneity of the dance and improvisation in the music into formalised treatments which still, particularly in the case of the Dance Theatre, retain to a remarkable extent the intensity of the original. Performances of these two groups offer the best chance for visitors to experience authentic, albeit second hand, Jamaican folk culture.

A recent development has been the emergence of a distinct **Rastafarian** music, spearheaded by a drumming and instrumental group rejoicing in the title *Count Ossie and the Mystic Revelation of the Rastafari.*

Sport. Cricket is king, and all over the island during the cricket season one hears the crack of bat on ball. When a Test Match is on, commerce slows, if it does not stop entirely, as the population crouches over transistor radios, or walks or cycles with them held against their ears. Jamaica usually contributes two or three players to the West Indies test side, and there is intense inter-territory rivalry to get players into the team. Cricket, after the English language, is the great unifying factor among the countries of the former British West Indies.

Horse racing is almost as popular as cricket, chiefly for the opportunities of gambling it provides.

Football is popular and entirely amateur, with most interest centred on the inter-High School games. **Athletics** is not as popular as it ought to be, considering the many fine runners Jamaica has produced, and other fringe sports are hockey, swimming, fishing, sailing, and last but certainly not least – dominoes, played in every rum shop on the island. Sports for visitors include **golf**, with eleven courses scattered over the island, ranging in price from Tryall, near Montego Bay in the luxury bracket, to Constant Spring in Kingston in (by comparison) the bargain basement. Another predominantly 'visitor sport' is **deep sea fishing**, for marlin, sailfish, wahoo, tuna etc. The main centres are Port Antonio and Montego Bay. More adventurous and/or penurious types may tackle the fish on their own ground, using a spear gun around the island's many reefs.

17

Spelunking. The greater part of Jamaica is soft limestone rock which has been carved out in places by present and former underground rivers to form vast caves. Two of the more accessible of them, Runaway Bay and Nonsuch near Port Antonio, may be conveniently toured on payment of a non-returnable deposit. Many others, however, even more spectacular and impressive, are farther from the beaten track, and require helmets, lamps, (sometimes ladders), and guidance for the visit. The vastness of some of the chambers and the fantastic shapes of the stalagmites and stalactites make the effort well worth while. Notable caves are at Windsor in Trelawny, Oxford near Balaclava, and Jackson's Bay near Lionel Town in Clarendon. Information can be had from the **Jamaican Caving Club**, contactable through the Tourist Board. In case you are wondering, spelunking is what spelologists do.

Spelunking in Windsor Cave, Trelawny

PAST

Jamaica's short history encompasses almost the entire spectrum of the human condition. From the Eden-like existence of the original gentle inhabitants in their tropical paradise, through their genocide by invaders, through slavery, slave uprisings and harsh repressions, piracy and plantocracy, colonialism and independence, floods, hurricane and earthquake – this small island has, within four hundred years, experienced them all.

Arawaks. When Colombus landed in Jamaica in 1494, the island was inhabited by a race of Indians, whom he described as being neither black nor white. They were a gentle people occupied mainly in primitive agriculture and fishing and they showed a shy hospitality to the newcomers. They were the Arawaks, members of the Amerindian group, related to the North American Indians, Mayas, Aztecs and Caribs, and they had reached Jamaica

18

from the mainland of South America by way of the chain of Islands known as the Lesser Antilles. After a century of Spanish rule, they had been exterminated by slaughter, overwork and disease, having no resistance to imported infections such as smallpox. Arawak skeletons which have been unearthed show them to have been short in stature, similar to related Indians who still live in the Orinoco region of South America, where Arawak is still spoken. They appear to have lived in small villages of circular thatched huts (*bohios*, still seen today in Cuba) situated on hills near to the coast, and to have eaten mainly shellfish, lizards (iguanas), and the coney, a larger cousin to the rat. They made bread from the poisonous cassava (manioc) root, and smoked tobacco. The many Arawak artifacts which have been excavated, mostly simple vessels and little god-figures (*zemis*) in stone or unglazed pottery, plus some primitive rock carvings around caves, indicate a civilisation not much advanced beyond the stone age. They were, however, very skilled in building and sailing dug-out canoes of the type still used by Jamaican fishermen.

The Institute of Jamaica has a large collection of Arawak relics, while an Arawak Museum built in the shape of a *bohio* on the site of an excavated Arawak settlement at White Marl (between Kingston and Spanish Town) has many more, and a smaller private collection is on display at the fine old greathouse of Iter Boreale near Annotto Bay.

Although extinct, the Arawaks are remembered in Jamaica by the two Indian supporters of the national coat of arms, and in the place names of Arawak origin such as *Liguanea, Gunboat Beach* (from Guanaboa) and, of course, *Jamaica*, their beloved 'land of wood and water'. They are commemorated also by many words of Arawak origin in the English language, such as tobacco, potato, hurricane, hammock, maize, barbecue, cannibal, and canoe.

Spanish. The first Spanish settlement in Jamaica was at Santa Gloria (now St Ann's Bay) where Diego Columbus founded the township of New Seville in 1509; his father Christopher Columbus had first sighted the island during his second voyage to the New World in 1494, and had spent a year of

Fountain in Savanna-la-Mar

enforced exile there in 1502 awaiting rescue after his ships the *Capitana* and the *Santiago* had had to be run aground, rotten and leaking, and with supplies exhausted. Their wrecks have recently been located by marine archaeologists in the waters of St Ann's Bay. New Seville proved to be an unhealthy site, as the settlers and their children succumbed rapidly to a variety of diseases, and after twenty five years the capital was moved to a site on the Rio Cobre near the south coast and named *Villa de la Vega*. At the height of Jamaica's 150 years of Spanish rule the capital boasted a Franciscan monastery, several churches, and perhaps 500 houses. As capital and a town of standing, it was paid the honour of being repeatedly sacked and burnt by a succession of adventurers and privateers, such as Sir Anthony Shirley in 1596 and Captain William Jackson in 1643.

Possessing no gold, Jamaica was used as a

source and reserve of food and provisions for the treasure ships plying between Spain and the Conquistadores in South America, who had recently vanquished, and were now plundering the riches of, Mexico and Peru. Having successfully exterminated the indigenous supply of free labour, the Arawaks, the Spaniards had to find an alternative. The problem was solved by importing slaves from Africa, and thus, unwittingly, the foundation stone of modern Jamaican society was laid. Let it be said, however, that the Spanish concept of slavery appears to have been much more liberal than that of the following British, as Spanish slaves were paid for their labour, and could in fact earn their freedom.

After the capture of Jamaica by the English in 1655 and the departure of most of the Spanish population to Cuba, a small force of Spaniards and free negroes under Don Cristobal Isassi carried on a spirited campaign of guerilla warfare from the mountains against the English. They were finally defeated, in a bitter battle, by the English under the command of Edward d'Oyley. Thus ended the Spanish chapter in Jamaica's history. Few physical relics of the Spaniards have survived, but the period has left a legacy of place names such as *Santa Cruz, Port Antonio, Savanna-la-Mar, Yallahs, Mount Diabolo, Negril (Negrillo), Port Morant (Puerto Morante), Port Maria, Oracabessa, Rio Grande, Rio Cobre, Rio Minho, Rio Bueno, Rio Cabritto, etc.*

English. Jamaica became an English possession by accident. Oliver Cromwell, as part of his great 'Western Design' to wrest control of the Caribbean from papist Spain, sent an expedition under the joint command of Admiral Sir William Penn and General Robert Venables, to capture the island of Hispaniola, (now Haiti). There, at Santo Domingo, they were decisively defeated, losing one third of their force in the attack. To salvage something from the debacle, Penn and Venables decided to attack Jamaica, known to be ill-defended. They sailed into the now Kingston Harbour on 10 May 1655, anchored off Caguaya and attacked Villa de la Vega, whose governor surrendered immediately, in return for safe passage for the

Spanish settlers to Cuba and Hispaniola. After Isassi's five years of guerilla warfare, the island was controlled by the English, apart from colonies of ex-Spanish Negroes who had established themselves in the least accessible areas of the island. These Maroons (from the Spanish *Cimarron*, meaning wild, untamed) harried the English settlements for many years, until a peace treaty in 1739 guaranteed them a large measure of independence. (See page 67 for a more detailed account). *Villa (later St Jago) de la Vega* was established as capital of the new colony, its title eventually changed to *Spanish Town*. England's claim to Jamaica was confirmed by the Treaty of Madrid in 1670.

Two factors now directed the nature of Jamaica's development. These were piracy and sugar.

The Buccaneers. From their rape and plunder of the ancient Aztec and Inca civilisations, the Spaniards were shipping vast fortunes in gold, silver and precious stones to Spain. This wealth had, of necessity, to pass through the Caribbean, which inspired a number of local 'spin-off' industries, such as smuggling, buccaneering, freebooting, privateering and marauding, whose rich pickings attracted to the area as unlovely a mob as ever gathered anywhere. The original buccaneers were international riff-raff who inhabited the north west forests of Hispaniola, where they hunted wild pigs and cattle, trading the meat, hides, lard etc., to passing ships for some of the booty that these vessels carried. From their method of preserving the meat by drying it in strips over a wooden frame called a *boucan* they derived the name *buccaneers*. The Spaniards forced them to leave Hispaniola and take refuge on the small island of Tortuga off the north coast. There they formed the 'Confederacy of the Brethren of the Coast' and took to sea in captured Spanish ships. Now, by intercepting Spanish galleons and stealing the booty, as opposed to trading boucan meat for it, they were elevated to the role of freebooters. Later, when they had developed formidable, well armed fleets, the European powers would give them commissions known as *letters of marque* conferring on them quasi-

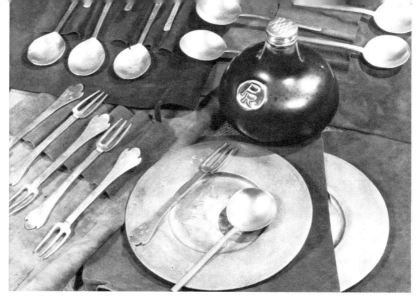

*Tudor and Spanish relics reclaimed from sea
(Devon House)*

naval status and promoting them to privateers. As they became more powerful and organised, the privateers could, and did, form fleets and small armies for the purpose of marauding, i.e. attacking the larger towns of the Caribbean. They could thus be useful to the European powers, who stimulated privateer fleets to attack the possessions of hostile countries. Perhaps the most outstanding operator was Henry Morgan. Morgan, the son of a Welsh farmer, served his pirate-ship with the Brethren in Tortuga, rose to command a ship and came to Jamaica, where Governor Modyford gave him letters of marque to attack Spanish ships. After various highly successful forays against the Spaniards his final and most spectacular exploit was the destruction of the city of Panama and its large defending garrison in 1607. As the Peace Treaty of Madrid had just been signed Morgan and Modyford found themselves in trouble with the authorities at home, but their punishment was nominal, and their disgrace short lived. Modyford, after a comfortable spell in the Tower of London, returned to Jamaica as Chief Justice, while Morgan returned as a hero to a knighthood, and was later made Governor. In this capacity he presided over the end of the buccaneering era, and was responsible for sending many of his old colleagues to a swinging end on Gallows Point in Port Royal. Surely the classic case of poacher turned gamekeeper!

After Tortuga, the focal point for the buccaneers became the town built at the end of the long sand split called the *Palisadoes* which shields Kingston Harbour. Named **Port Royal**, to acknowledge the Restoration of the monarchy, it was heavily fortified and offered a good deep water harbour for ships' anchorage and repair. It also provided a market for booty and opportunities for the Brethren to relax a little in debauchery of all kinds.

With the influx of buccaneers, Port Royal gained notoriety as 'the wickedest city in the world'. Unfortunately, all good things must come to an end, and Port Royal's came on 7 June 1692, when, during a savage and sudden earthquake, most of the town slid gracefully under the sea. It was at this time, a city of over 1 000 brick and timber houses, Governor's residence, several churches, a prison, three daily markets, and even 'a house of correction for lazy strumpets'. The town was ringed by no less than six forts, of which Fort Charles alone boasted thirty eight cannon. Over two thousand people are estimated to have met their deaths by falling masonry, being swallowed in fissures, drowning, or by various combinations of these. A Frenchman called Lewis Galdy had a miraculous escape, being swallowed by a fissure,

Fort Charles, Port Royal, oldest relic of English Jamaica

then being forced back out by a subsequent shock into the sea, where he saved himself by swimming to a boat. His grave may be seen in the churchyard of St Peter's Church, Port Royal.

After this disaster, Port Royal painfully gathered the threads together again, defeated attempts by Kingston to replace her as 'Queen of the Sea', and rose again from the ruins. Most of the buildings were wood, this being more resistant to earthquake. Unfortunately, it is non-resistant to fire, and a disastrous outbreak in 1704 reduced the town to ashes. Again it was rebuilt, and the privateers and men-o'-war returned. However, the following forty years were marked by a series of hurricanes, each leaving the exposed town further reduced in size and stature. Among the pirates who frequented the town during the post earthquake years were *Blackbeard* (Edward Teach), who is said to have fought with fuses burning in his matted hair and beard, and *'Calico Jack' Rackham*, who had the distinction of having two women

pirates, Anne Bonney and Mary Read among his crew. Captured in Negril Bay after a fight in which the ladies were reported to have fought hardest of all, Rackham met his end on Gallows Point, and his remains were hung on the Cay which now bears his name. The women escaped death on pleas of pregnancy. As piracy declined, use of Port Royal as a naval station grew, and a succession of Britain's famous admirals served there. Benbow, who died there from wounds, Hood, Rodney, and Nelson, who, as a captain of twenty one, had command of the battery at Fort Charles while awaiting an expected French invasion. It continued to be occupied and fortified until 1907, when another earthquake devastated the port, and effectively terminated its use as a naval station. Port Royal's 200-year battle with nature was over.

Sugar and Slaves. Prior to sugar's 'Flood Tide' in the eighteenth century, the majority of European settlers in Jamaica were smallholders or indentured labourers, bound by contract to work for several years in return for their passage to the colony and the prospect of free land at the end of their indenture period. The growing, reaping and milling of sugar cane needed a vast amount of labour, and when the labour needs of the booming sugar plantations could not be met, the planters turned to the source of man-power used for over 100 years by Portuguese and Spaniards – Africa.

The Portuguese had established slave stations or *barracoons* on the West Coast of Africa as early as 1490, to supply slaves to their colony in Brazil. As the 'indispensable handmaid of the sugar industry' the slave trade was soon booming. In 1673 the popula-tion of Jamaica was 7 700 whites (many of them recent emigrants from Barbados) and 9 500 blacks. Fifty years later the white population was essentially the same, whilst the number of negro slaves had risen to 74 000; by 1800 it had soared to over 300 000. The price of slaves rose with in-creasing demand, averaging £25 each in 1700 and rising to £50 in 1730. Often payment was made in sugar or rum, with a ton of sugar being the average price for a male slave. In 1807, the last year of the British slave trade, 40 000 slaves were shipped from Africa to the British West Indies.

The majority of slaves were in the field-work gangs, which did the heavy and un-pleasant tasks of digging fields to plant the cane, then cutting it at harvest and trans-porting it to the factory. Next in unpopu-larity came labour in the factory, grinding the cane, boiling the sugar in the heat and steam of the boiling house, and moving the heavy hogshead barrels to and from the curing house. Two classes of slaves were privileged inasmuch as they did not have to do any backbreaking field or factory work. These were the domestic servants at the great house and the skilled craftsmen. The planters brought out craftsmen from Europe to teach selected slaves the arts of masonry, carpentry, etc. and the legacy of high quality stonework, woodwork and furniture shows how well they learned.

Revolt and Emancipation. The planters were eventually greatly outnumbered by the slaves and consequently lived in constant fear of slave uprisings. It was an unhappy society, fearful on one side, resentful on the other, with the planters as much prisoners of it as the slaves. Most of the larger Jamaican planters lived in Britain, and it was the ambition of their managers and overseers to

British guns from the deep

earn enough money to be able to retire there also.

On occasions, the slaves' misery and frustration caused their usual passive resistance to erupt into open rebellion, of which Jamaica had a higher incidence than any other colony. Between 1706 and Emancipation in 1834 there were numerous revolts of greater or less importance, inevitably suppressed and inevitably followed by punishments of the most horrible and repressive kind.

Emancipation, in 1834, following the British Parliament's recognition of the humanitarian and economic wrongs of slavery, was a triumph for the dedicated band of men led by Wilberforce, Clarkson and Sharpe, who had campaigned for over forty years. They were supported in Jamaica by a group of non-conformist missionaries, prominent among whom were the Reverends Knibb, Phillipo and Burchell. The Jamaican Assembly and the planters fought abolition tooth and nail, and missionaries who preached to the slaves were subjected to a campaign of terror which included the burning of their churches. Compensation at roughly £27 per adult and £4 per child slave was paid to the Jamaican planters by the British Government, and a three year period of apprenticeship was enforced during which the ex-slaves did paid work for their former owners. After this most of them wanted nothing further to do with the estates and settled whatever free lands they could find as smallholders. Their troubles were by no means over, however; nothing was done to help them economically, they were to all intents and purposes without the vote, and received scant justice in the courts. Their grievances came to a head in the Morant Bay Rebellion of 1865. This rebellion, although promptly and brutally suppressed, led to subsequent far-reaching reforms. (See page 62 for a fuller account).

The rise of the sugar industry in the Caribbean changed the course of history here, in Europe, and even in Africa. It caused the movement of peoples on a vast scale and over great distances, spread the Negro race throughout the New World, gave rise to cruelty which was terrible even in such a savage age, and eventually it spelt the end of a system of bondage as old as the human race.

PRACTICAL

Getting There. Jamaica is served by numerous flights from the US, Canada, and Britain. On some round trips offered by the air lines it is possible to make up to four stopovers, allowing for interesting side excursions. Some very good value package holidays are available from various travel agents.

For those who prefer, and can afford, to travel by sea, there are both fruit and banana boats and cruise ships which call regularly.

Entering: British and Commonwealth citizens require no visa for Jamaica, and Americans and Canadians do not even require passports if they are coming on holiday. It is necessary to have a return ticket to show that you have the intention and means to leave. A **smallpox vaccination** is the only health certificate required, but anyone arriving without one will be quickly and painlessly vaccinated in the airport. **Customs** allowances are similar to those in most other countries, but are seldom rigorously applied to visitors.

Currency is the **Jamaican dollar** which is related to the US dollar. The rate at time of going to press is J$1.00 = US$1.10; the £1 sterling buys roughly J$2.17. Both figures may well be different by the time this book is in print! In and around Montego Bay more US Dollars are used than Jamaican, and one should check in which currency prices are quoted before buying.

Precautions — all Jamaican water is safe to drink, so no tablets against tourist tummy are necessary. You should, however, guard against getting too much sun, especially on the beach, by keeping your head covered and by applying one of the many sun oils or creams available.

Another wise precaution is to use an **anti-insect** spray, as mosquitos or sand flies can make life miserable. The latter are occasionally aggressive on the beaches.

FOOD Jamaican cuisine reflects the cosmopolitan nature of the island's society, with European, African, Chinese and Indian influences all contributing. With such a wide variety of vegetables, fruits and seafood readily available, the food may be expected to be exotic, and it is. A characteristic is spiciness, with liberal use of the plentiful local hot peppers, ginger and spices. Standard European/American dishes, from Wiener Schnitzel to hamburgers, are to be found on most menus, but for the less timid visitor, much of the pleasure in the visit will be derived from seeking out and trying the local dishes.

In Jamaica, as in most other countries, the truly national dishes have been discovered and developed by the poorer people as methods of spinning out a few cents worth of meat or fish protein into a filling meal. Lest some of the fruits and vegetables encountered be strange, a short glossary may prove helpful.

Vegetables.

green bananas	picked before fully ripe and boiled or fried.
plantain	larger, savoury cousin of the banana, boiled or fried.
cho-cho	pear-shaped vegetable with prickly skin, grows on a vine – flesh reminiscent of marrow.
breadfruit	round green fruit with bumpy exterior, served boiled or fried; tastes as its name suggests.
callaloo	not unlike spinach.
cassava	tuber contains cyanide when raw, but when well washed and ground is used as flour to make bammie (savoury flat cakes). An old Arawack favourite.
yams, yampies, dasheen cocos	tubers of the same family; usually boiled and served as carbohydrate.
irish potato	the common spud, so called to distinguish it from the sweet potato.

Fruits. In addition to those too well-known to need explaining, there are:

sweet sop	rough skinned fruits containing many seeds, whose pulpy flesh is
sour sop	served as a desert or made into a drink with milk.
paw paw	(strictly papaya) resembles a cross between melon and mango, served in slices for breakfast or dessert, usually with a squeeze of lime.
mango	green fruit with orange flesh surrounding a single large stone. The common variety (hairy mango) is fibrous and stringy, but the most popular varieties, Julie, Bombay, and No. 11 are delicious and fibre free.
naseberry	(sapodilla) a small round brown fruit whose jelly-like flesh has a peculiar almost burnt taste.

Seafood. For an island set in seas teeming with fish, Jamaica makes surprisingly little use of them in cuisine. They range from sharks to sprats, and come in all colours of the rainbow, although the meat when served is usually white and succulent. The most common are the various snappers (yellowtail, blackfin, silk, etc.), jacks, and the razor-toothed king fish, which is normally served in cross-sectioned steaks. Other table fish are groupers, grunts, bonitos, parrots, butters, surgeons, and even that tiger of the sea, the barracuda. Turtle steaks were formerly very common in Jamaica, but now are less so due to overfishing and to the stealing of turtle eggs from the beaches where they are laid.

Fish Dishes include such specialities as:

shrimp and lobster (not true lobster but the clawless spiny lobster)	plentiful and served in the usual variety of ways.
salt fish and ackee	the national dish, delicious and inexpensive. The yellow arilli of the ackee when cooked resemble scrambled egg; fried with onions and peppers etc. it makes a perfect complement to soaked and boiled cod fish flakes. Excellent for breakfast.
stuffed crabs	uses green land crabs, whose delicately flavoured meat is chopped, mixed with breadcrumbs, onions and spices, and baked in the shell. Usually served as an entree.
run-down fish	generally mackerel or salt fish boiled in coconut milk with onions peppers etc. to a mush. Tastes better than it sounds.
stamp and go	salt fish in batter dropped by the tablespoon into hot fat, forming fritters which are served as an entree or as a snack eaten with the fingers.
solomon gundy	spiced pickled herring, used as sandwich filling or as hors d'oeuvres.

Meats include a speciality called *jerk pork*, which is described under Boston Bay, Portland (page 65), and is almost peculiar to that area; *curried goat* with the inevitable **pepper** thrown in (goats seem to be amazingly bony animals); and *pigeon*, during the shooting season, is available in the better restaurants. Most meat and fish dishes are accompanied by *rice and peas* (red beans), the popularity of which is acknowledged in its nickname 'Jamaica's coat of arms'. The standard snack is a *meat pattie*, which is meat and breadcrumbs enclosed in a flap of pastry. Pepper content varies inversely with meat!

Desserts and sweets to tickle your fancy are:

matrimony	a blend of orange segments with star apple pulp in cream.
grilled bananas	cooked in their skins and served with rum and lime.
sweet potato pudding	a stodgy dumpling-like creation, which can be greatly improved by liberal additions of rum.
guava cheese	a rubbery confection made by boiling down strained ripe guavas with sugar.

Drink. Jamaica is an inebriate's paradise, with a large variety of noggins, from beer to bay rum, available at reasonable prices. Pride of place goes, of course, to rum, and rightly so, as many fine brands are available. Do not confuse the various weird and wonderful dark products sold as Jamaican rum in Europe with the product consumed by Jamaicans. The trend in Jamaica is to lighter, less aromatic rums; among the current favourites are *Appleton Special, Gold Label* and *Charley's*. Rum is mixed with a variety of 'chasers' such as dry ginger ale, or coconut water (the juice from young coconuts, and different from the milk of the mature nut). Both are good complements to rum, being delicate enough not to drown the flavour. Coca Cola is a chaser for those who want the sensation of rum without its taste. The most popular drink with poorer Jamaicans is white overproof rum, which will blister paintwork. *Rum Punch* (or *Planter's Punch*) is a term used to cover a multitude of sins, and many local concoctions involve overproof rum plus a fluorescent pink raspberry syrup. They are vile. True punch consists of:

> One of sour (one part juice from green limes)
> Two of sweet (two parts clear sugar syrup)
> Three of strong (three parts brown rum)
> Four of weak (four parts water and crushed ice)

add a little nutmeg on the surface and suck it down.

'Jerk' pork cooked over burning coals

A range of other distilled drink is made locally under licence, including gin, vodka, and a selection of liqueurs. They are consequently much cheaper than imported spirits, and of equivalent quality. Jamaican **liqueurs** include *Tia Maria*, made from Blue Mountain coffee; *Pimento Dram*, an old Jamaican tipple, and one where the mature home-made infusion, if you can get it, is usually much better than the somewhat sickly commercial product. *Rumona* is a liqueur of indeterminate flavour based, as the name suggests, on rum.

Red Stripe Beer, the local lager, is very good, and also very strong. After exercising a benign monopoly for many years, Red Stripe now share the market with Guinness, who have built a local brewery. In addition to these many locally-produced drinks, it is possible to obtain virtually any foreign beverage; English, Scottish, German, Dutch and American beers; French, German, and Italian wines; sherries and port.

With such a profusion of fruits growing locally, there are many **fruit juices** to choose from, such as orange, grapefruit, ortanique, pineapple, plus many others more exotic, including sour sop, a prickly green fruit, which is blended with milk; paw paw nectar and mango nectar, both rather thickly pleasant, and tamarind nectar an excellent thirst quencher. Popular **non-fruit drinks** are coconut water, drunk straight out of the nut (the vendor chops an end off with his machete) and last but not least, sugar cane juice, a greenish sweet liquid crushed from the cane, and sometimes ginger flavoured.

Blue Mountain Coffee is the most expensive in the world, and in great demand in most coffee drinking countries, which perhaps explains why it is almost impossible to buy in Jamaica. It is prized as a blending coffee, and, taken alone, has a strong, almost harsh flavour. However, its taste once acquired, makes most other coffees seem bland by comparison. It can be bought as roasted beans at *Magic Kitchen* in Tropical Plaza, off Half-Way Tree Road, Kingston. Instant coffees sold and served as Blue Mountain Coffee are blends of no more than 10% with 90% other coffees (usually imported).

Eating out. Most hotels offer meals to non-residents, and there exists a wide range of restaurants at all levels. The following, which is a purely personal selection, indicates establishments which are noteworthy either for quality or good value. Places mentioned elsewhere in the guide have been omitted from this section.

27

Kingston

Quality restaurants, in roughly descending order of price, include:

Swiss Chalet, Holbourn Road
(off Trafalgar Road)

regarded as the best of the 'in-town' restaurants, specialising in continental cuisine.

Terra Nova, 17 Waterloo Road

in the same style as above but slightly cheaper.

The Mill, Manor Park Plaza
(off Constant Spring Road)

has a beautiful spacious setting around an old mill wheel; good food.

Continental, 6 Worthington Avenue
(off Trafalgar Road)

a homely family-run concern, similar to above but less spacious.

Casa Monte, Old Stony Hill Road
(well signposted)

enjoys a panoramic view of Kingston and has an excellent barbecue, with music, on Friday nights.

Devon House, corner of Hope Road
and Waterloo Road

specialises in Jamaican food in a pleasant if affected seventeenth-century Port Royal setting. Excellent buffet dinner (Wednesday) and barbecue dinner (Saturday) both with calypso band.

Nyam and Scram (Quick service or take away) lunches are available at:

Green Gables, 6 Cargill Avenue
(off Half Way Tree Road)

fish and chips, good cold plate, and draught beers in its pub.

The Indies Pub, beyond Swiss
Chalet on opposite side of
Holbourn Road.

offers similar fare, plus pizza as a special; open 11 a.m. until 11.30 p.m.

Four Seasons, Ruthven Road
(between Half Way Tree Road and
Trafalgar Road)

offers good low-cost hot buffet lunch.

House of Chen, 69 Knutsford Boulevard
New Kingston

Chinese businessman's-lunch amid luxurious surroundings.

Birdcage, Ruthven Road
(behind Sutton Court)

a slightly more leisurely and expensive poolside lunch.

Downtown, moderate meals may be had at *Paul's*, on Harbour Street, *Cathay* (Chinese) at 88 Orange Street (below Parade), or one can have reasonably priced unpretentious food in a spartan atmosphere at the *British Sailor's Society*, near the bottom of Duke Street (popular with matelots and also local expatriate office workers.

Kingston has many Chinese restaurants; the following give good value for money:
> *Mee-Mee*, Northside Plaza, behind Barclay's Bank, at Liguanea
> *Golden Dragon* Mona Plaza, off Mona Road
> *Joongwah*, small plaza beside Liguanea traffic lights
> *House of Chen*, Knutsford Boulevard, New Kingston.

Montego Bay

Quality restaurants recommended are:

Miranda Hill, off Queen's Drive overlooking the bay
The Town House, 16 Church Street – good food in an old-world atmosphere.
The Calabash, Queen's Drive

Nyam and Scram is obtainable at:

Pelican Grill, Gloucester Avenue, near the hospital
The Admiral's Inn, Upper Deck Hotel – daily business-man's lunch.

In other areas are:

Mandeville, *Bill Laurie's Steak House*, Perth Road, continuation of Caledonia Road, after the turn (right) to Black River from Kingston. It offers reasonably priced food in a pub atmosphere.
Spanish Town, *Happy Hunter*, from Kingston, past the prison on left-hand side of the main road on corner. Upstairs bar and restaurant.
May Pen, *Aquarius*, on main western road (left) leaving town. Upstairs bar and restaurant.
Negril, *Negril Sands*, halfway along the beach, and the *Yacht Club* (in Negril village). Both specialise in sea-food at moderate prices.
East Coast, *Ports of Call*, Long Bay for good, cheap sea food.

Entertainment. Most of the following relates to Kingston, although plays are occasionally staged in provincial centres; hotels all over the island have floor shows and bands, and cinemas are to be found in all population centres.

Theatre. Kingston has four, being in order of size *Ward Theatre* (North Parade) *Little Theatre* (Tom Redcam Drive, near the National Stadium) *Creative Arts Centre* (University Campus) and the *Barn* (Norwood Avenue, off Oxford Road). All stage both imported and local plays, and the standard of local acting and production is surprisingly high.

Night life – shapely floor show

National Dance Company — 'Dialogue for Three'

Each year around Christmas is the local **pantomime**, a patois production of variable quality. Kingston boasts many cinemas; you are strongly advised to stick to *Carib, Regal, Odeon* and *Harbour View Drive-In*, as most of the others are in rough areas with a reputation for violence. For swingers, Kingston has two good discotheques, *Epiphany* (Spanish Court, New Kingston) and *Dizzy's* (Northside Plaza, above Matilda's Corner, left, with Barclays Bank on the corner).

Night Life. The larger hotels have resident bands and regular floor shows. In Kingston, *Sheraton* has a modern combo in its Jonkannoo Room, and Skyline has coloured costermongers, the *Pearly Kings*, in *The Pub*, (open buffet for 50c). Kingston also has many bars and 'clubs', these being bars with available women, whose company can be enjoyed on the premises (usually very grotty) or in the seclusion of your own hotel. Visitors wishing to explore the 'red light' districts are strongly advised to stick to the establishments described below; those who stray elsewhere stand an excellent chance of being robbed, beaten up, or worse. Clubs are constantly appearing and disappearing, but a number of hardy perennials are (in decreasing order of price and sophistication): *Queen of Hearts* (Oxford Terrace, off Old Hope Road, below Oxford Road); *Rhapsody* (below Cross Roads on Orange Street, in the little plaza at the junction with Alton Villa Road), which features some splendid black go-go dancers; *Bamboo* (top of Duke Street, on the right coming up) which has both calypso band and video juke box. *Beach Club*, better known as 'Joyce's', after the proprietress Miss Deere, an ageless lady of extensive vocabulary and uncertain temper who seems to know most of Kingston's male population, is sited near the harbour, due east of Harbour Street, on the corner of William and Hannah Streets. It is unpretentious and friendly. This indeed is a feature of the clubs and girls in Kingston's entertainment areas. Bottom of the club league, friendly and least pretentious of all, is *Millie's Fun Jug* (a short way up Mountain View Avenue on the left). Montego Bay has its equivalents of the above, and in peak periods, reinforcements are drafted in from Kingston.

Dunn's River Falls, a natural attraction (see page 74)

Day Life. Organised tours of Kingston and its surroundings are available (*Martins Tours*) as are guided tours of some plantations such as *Good Hope, Brimmer Hall, Runaway Plantation*, etc. Most hotels allow non-residents to use their swimming pool, and for children in Kingston, *Hope Gardens* contains a zoo with an adjacent fun fair.

Shopping. Tourist blurb makes much of Jamaica's **in bond** duty free shopping. Note however that the items purchased cannot be used in Jamaica, and are delivered to purchasers only on leaving the island. Any items such as cameras which are intended for use during the visit should be purchased duty free before leaving for Jamaica, in the airport or on board ship. The in bond shops offer a wide range of cameras, watches, radios, jewelry, perfumes and are located in downtown Kingston, Montego Bay, Ocho Rios etc. Storekeepers pay a large deposit to the government as security, and the system is well-organised.

For normal over-the-counter shopping, Jamaica is fairly expensive and lacks the tradition and wealth of handcrafts possessed by countries in say South America or Africa. Some items, however, are characteristically Jamaican and reasonable in price. **Wood carvings**, especially Rastafarian carvings of heads and figures, are usually good value, you should look for those carved from the very dense **Lignum vitae**, where the carvers often take cunning advantage of differences in colour in the wood grain to highlight aspects of the carving. Wood carvings are available in Kingston at Devon House, the Crafts Market and Hill's Gallery (99½ Harbour Street), and at roadside stalls all along the north coast, where some haggling will usually bring down the price. **Straw work** tends to be garish, but of late some tasteful straw items are slipping through and are best bought at the **Crafts Market**, as are beads, bamboo carvings, etc. **Jamaican embroidery** is very good and is reasonably priced. Colourful local scenes embellish linen dresses, towels, handkerchiefs etc., which have the additional advantage of being easily packed and carried. Jamaica Textiles Ltd., produce attractive locally designed and printed fabrics, with patterns based on Jamaican plants and flowers. Their factory and showroom may be visited east of May Pen on the road to Kingston, and they also have a small shop in Devon

31

House in Kingston. **Hand-dyed batik silks and cottons** are produced by Caribatik in their little factory (open to visitors) beside Fisherman's Inn outside Falmouth and sold there and at their other shops. **Paintings** by local artists are fairly high-priced and are sold in Kingston at the School of Art (11 North Street), the Contemporary Jamaican Artist's Gallery (17 Oxford Road), Hill's Gallery and Bolivar Gallery (Grove Road, off Half-Way-Tree Rd.). The latter two also sell antique **Jamaican prints and maps**, and Bolivar has a resident (a.m. only) silversmith who has produced a range of jewelry of original design. Moderately priced folios of facsimile old coloured prints of Jamaican scenes by the artists Kidd and Belisario are on sale in the Institute of Jamaica's sales kiosk at 12 East Street, and facsimiles of pewter cutlery and ceramic crockery recovered from sunken Port Royal are well produced by Things Jamaican for sale in their shops at Devon House, Manley and Sangster Airports and the Crafts Market.

Furniture is not the normal type of souvenir, but Things Jamaican also produce beautiful reproductions of antique mahogany pieces. Anyone passing through the little town of Highgate, south of Annotto Bay should visit the Society of Friends workshop there, where solid, simple furniture from local hardwood such as mahoe is sold very reasonably. While there, visit the nearby pottery showroom of an American couple, the Todds, for very high quality ceramics. Gems are more easily transported than chairs or vases, and **local semi-precious stones** are sold at Blue Mountain Gems, opposite to Holiday Inn, near Montego Bay, where visitors can see agates, jaspers etc., being cut and polished.

Transport

By Road. Jamaica's main road follows the coastline around the island, with many other roads crossing the island, linking the north and south coasts. The roads are paved and generally good, although dual carriageways are still a novelty. For seeing most of the island, the method of choice is by car, and many car hire firms are available (Hertz, Avis etc.). Some of the off-the-beaten-track routes suggested require a sturdy compact car such as a Volkswagen. When motoring, use the premium grade petrol (costs 50c/gallon) as the normal grade is pretty rough. Jamaicans drive on the left, as in Britain, and there is a competitiveness and unpredictability about some of their driving which makes every journey an adventure. Hand signals usually indicate that the driver is flicking ash from his cigarette, or has seen a friend. Taxis are plentiful in towns, and cost 30c for the first mile and 15c per mile thereafter. Between towns, travel is by bus or mini-bus, with the latter offering an irregular but frequent service. The bus terminus in Kingston is due north of the railway station, up Pechon Street, at the west end of Harbour Street. Another type of transport, not recommended except for the experience, is the gaily painted market truck, filled with seats to hold vast numbers.

By Air. There are over forty landing strips in Jamaica, dotting the island and making all parts quickly and easily accessible from the main towns. Three small airlines ply three and five-passenger planes between all landing ships. Jamaica Air Service have **regular daily flights** between Kingston, Mandeville (also Jamaica Air Taxi), **Montego Bay, Port Antonio** and Ocho Rios, while Jamaica Air Taxi and **Airways** offer a **taxi service** i.e. one, two or three passengers are the same price, it being the **plane plus pilot** you hire. They will **collect or drop** you at any airstrip, costs being e.g. $35 single $54 return Kingston to Port Antonio. The Kingston centre for such small **plane flights** is Tinson Pen Airport, near Newport West. Flights from Manley and Sangster Airports require a $2 government departure tax.

By Rail. Kingston has rail connections with Montego Bay and Port Antonio. Both carry single class local trains which stop frequently along the route to pick up passengers, goods, and a variety of livestock. Train travel affords an opportunity to relax and view the scenic interior of the island, and to travel like a local. Apart from being interesting, it is cheap; Kingston to Port Antonio is a mere 90c return. The Montego Bay route passes through the Appleton valley, then along the edge of the Cockpit Country, while the Port Antonio line follows a beautiful stretch of coastline for 35 miles after Annotto Bay.

The train times are:

Dept. Kingston	7.00		Arrive. Mo.Bay	11.25	(Daily)	
Dept. Kingston	10.05		Arrive. Mo Bay	17.55	(Mon to Sat)	
Dept. Kingston	15.45		Arrive. Mo Bay	20.00	(Daily)	
Dept. Kingston	7.25		Arrive. Pt. Ant.	10.45	(Sat, Sun)	
Dept. Kingston	13.30		Arrive. Pt. Ant.	18.40	(Mon to Sat)	
Dept. Kingston	16.15		Arrive. Pt. Ant.	19.40	(Daily)	
Dept. Mo Bay	6.45		Arrive. Kgn.	11.20	(Daily)	
Dept. Mo Bay	7.35		Arrive. Kgn.	14.50	(Mon to Sat)	
Dept. Mo Bay	15.30		Arrive. Kgn.	20.00	(Daily)	
Dept. Pt. Ant.	5.40		Arrive. Kgn.	9.05	(Daily)	
Dept. Pt. Ant.	6.30		Arrive. Kgn.	11.40	(Mon to Sat)	
Dept. Pt. Ant.	16.00		Arrive. Kgn.	19.40	(Sat, Sun)	

The **Governor's Coach** is a luxury tourist diesel train which, complete with calypso band and bar, runs daily from Montego Bay (leaves the station at 10 a.m.) along the edge of the Cockpits to Appleton, where a tour of the sugar factory (in croptime, January to June) and the famous distillery is included before returning to Montego Bay for 4 p.m. Cost, including lunch is $11.

Accommodation. The two main types of tourist accommodation are **hotels**, which offer either bed and breakfast or bed alone, and **cottages/resort villas** which are normally rented by the week but which can also be had for a single night if they are vacant. They are cheaper and more convenient for families or groups who want privacy and are prepared to look after themselves, although many cottages include the service of a cook/housekeeper in the rate. Some cottages, slightly more expensive, are sited almost on the beach. Some of the most modern hotels offer a combination of both types of accommodation, having a central hotel building with restaurant, saloon, tennis courts etc. surrounded by a colony of individual cottages each with its own cooking facilities. Examples are Dragon Bay, Goblin Hill and Trident on the east coast, and Club Caribbean, Silver Sands and Ironshore on the north coast.

The price of most accommodation rises from 50 to 100% during the tourist season which runs from 16 December until 15 April, but most north coast hotels offer 25% reductions to those claiming to be Jamaican residents. The decision whether to book in advance must be personal: Kingston is often fully booked, but it is usually possible to get hotel or cottage accommodation in other parts of the island without booking. Unfortunately, Jamaica is short of private *bed and breakfast* houses or an equivalent of the European *pension*, but some **guest houses** do exist, also some small hotels whose rates are cheap by island standards. Some purely personal recommendations are:

Kingston
Abahati, Indies Pub and Guest House, Mayfair, Green Gables, Sandhurst, Sutton Place.

Montego Bay – Upper Deck, Palm Beach, Beach View, Harvey Beach, Blue Harbour

East Coast – De Montevin Lodge, Bonnie View, Goblin Hill, Ports of Call, Long Bay Beach

South Coast – Hendon House (Sav-la-Mar), Bluefields Great House, Treasure Beach

Mandeville – Astra, Braemar

West Coast – Tamarind Lodge (nr. Lucea), **Saxham** Guest House (E. of Green Island), Pimento Cove, 4 miles west of Lucea

Addresses are given in the list of hotels, pages 89 to 94.

KINGSTON

THE TRIANGLE OF HISTORY

Area 1   **KINGSTON, PORT ROYAL, SPANISH TOWN**

KINGSTON, in spite of its magnificent natural setting, is not a beautiful town, giving an impression from the air of a sprawling jumble of heterogeneous buildings interspersed with trees. The older 'downtown' area still shows signs of being planned as an entity, being laid out in the Spanish 'gridiron' tradition around a square central park, but most of the rest appears to be the result of speculative builders having had a free hand. The city consists largely of a core of picturesque slums, once the homes of the wealthy who have now moved out to the suburbs, surrounded by banal, well maintained bungalows. The fashionable part of town, built on the 1 400 ft. high Long Mountain, is Beverley Hills, as varied a collection of architectural styles and extravaganza as one can find anywhere. Barely 100 yards from this opulence, and in many other large areas of Kingston, the vast mass of less affluent members of society exist in overcrowded shanties, sharing the dirt roads between them with pigs, goats, and starving mongrels. Bungaloid growths are pushing out along the coast and up into the foothills of the Blue Mountains, but this trend is partially offset by the many fine modern buildings which have been built. Nor have the attractive old survivors of earthquakes, fires and hurricanes been neglected, and some skilful pieces of restoration and preservation have been carried out. Kingston's vitality stems largely from the fact that it is a busy port, almost unique in that ocean-going ships can berth within 100 yards of some of its main streets, enriching the skyline with their contribution of masts and funnels. The eastern side of the harbour is formed by the Palisadoes, the ten-mile sandbar housing the busy **Norman Manley International Airport**, and terminating in Port Royal. In its people as in its buildings, Kingston is a city of contrasts — Negroid, Caucasian, Semitic and Mongoloid features and colours mingle, and blend in the infinite number of racial mixtures which Jamaica has produced. A less pleasant contrast is seen between downtown beggars, and wealthy businessmen whose large American cars are a status symbol completely unsuited to Jamaican roads. The city's growing population, over half a million in 1971, is expected to reach 700 000 by 1975, due to a combination of the high birthrate and an influx of people from country districts looking for work.

The capital, in addition to housing the seats of Government and justice, has, on its outskirts, the University of the West Indies and the Hope Botanical Garden. It has neither opera house nor concert hall, but its several theatres support an active and high quality drama-and-dance programme. The National Stadium is a modern and impressive complex which is the focal point of Jamaica's sports life. Kingston's 'sporting life' is quite another thing, and has its focal point(s) in the bars and clubs downtown, which have female satellites who can only be described as super-friendly. The city offers more prosaic tourist services in the form of several first-class hotels and excellent duty-free *in-bond* shopping.

ROUTES

OLD KINGSTON The great majority of visitors to Kingston arrive at **Norman Manley Airport** so it is convenient to approach the town from this direction. From the airport the road follows the narrow Palisadoes (so-called because of the defensive fencework originally erected) sandspit, passing the popular **Gunboat and Buccaneer** beaches on the left and within a few yards of a rusting shipwreck on the right. The dramatic view encompasses the entire spread of Kingston to the left, and the sweep of the Blue Mountains receding into St

Thomas on the right. The hill whose low bulk is directly ahead is **Long Mountain**, a rocky finger projecting deep into Kingston, and the round stone structure half-way up is a Martello Tower built in 1803 as a fortress against possible French invasion and similar to those built along the English coast at the time. The road meets the mainland at a roundabout, turning left for Kingston, past the large middle-class housing scheme of **Harbour View** on the right. The approach to the capital is, unfortunately, a singularly

Kingston shopping in King Street

magazine is the only building still standing, although the foundations of the Captain's House, barracks for 200 men, and kitchen are still visible. Until recently the sea washed against the walls and the main road to Kingston passed through the fortified gate. The road continues as the *Windward Road* (the eastern end of the island was formerly given the nautical title of Windward) through one of Kingston's most depressing areas of run-down houses, shacks and teeming shops.

At the first set of traffic lights, *Mountain View Avenue* goes right, bypassing the downtown area, to the National Stadium, New Kingston, Liguanea and Mona. The Windward Road continues to the third cross-roads where on the right *South Camp Road* goes up to Cross Roads, passing en route Up Park Camp, depot of the Jamaica Defence Force. On the left is the **General Penitentiary**, near the water's edge and surrounded by the squalor and sleazy bars of **Rae Town**. On entering Central Kingston, the Windward Road changes its name to East Queen Street, crosses the gridiron of the older part of the town and terminates on the east side of the central Parade, whose enclosed nondescript park has statues of **Norman Manley** and **Sir Alexander Bustamante** on the north and south sides respectively. From the top of *King Street* round the west side of the square, the sidewalks and doorways house a free-for-all of stalls and vendors selling everything from bananas to ball-point pens. On the north side of the square is the **Ward Theatre**, the largest in Jamaica, donated to the community by Colonel Charles Ward, a former owner of J. Wray & Nephew, Jamaica's largest rum manufacturers. The statue in the road nearby is Norman Manley. The rather forbidding brick building on the corner of East Queen Street is Coke Chapel, named after a Methodist preacher, and the church whose stately square tower graces the corner of King Street and South Parade is **Kingston Parish Church**, built on the site of the original which was destroyed in the 1907 earthquake. It contains the tomb of Admiral Benbow, mortally wounded in 1702 during the battle of Santa Marta against duCasse, the French equivalent of Henry Morgan (see p 21). The church also contains three wall memorials by

uninspiring one, passing a cement works, an oil bunkering terminal, a flour mill, and a series of petrol stations. The one patch of interest in this industrial sprawl is the ruin of **Rock Fort** in the shadow of the monolithic cement works. Sited between the sheer sides of Long Mountain and the sea, Rock Fort was built in 1792 on the site of a 1694 fortress, to command the eastern approaches to Kingston. Although neglected and deserted, the fort is remarkably well preserved, and still has almost its full complement of cannon, some of which project over the road, and all of which now have a generous coating of cement. It is possible to park at the side below the fort and to browse around. The

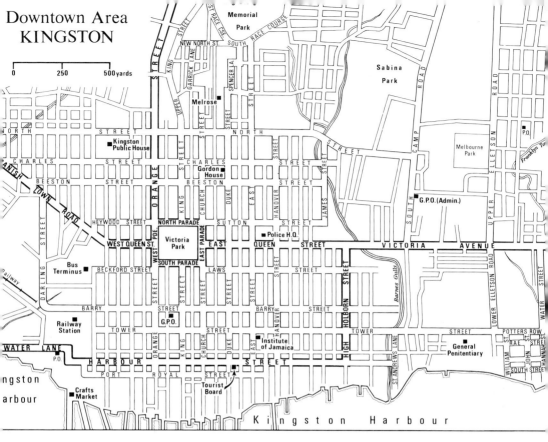

John Bacon, the leading English sculptor of his day. South from Parade runs *King Street* the main shopping street in Kingston. On it are found the **General Post Office** on the right, opposite the more pleasantly proportioned **Law Courts** situated behind a little plaza. In front of the G.P.O. is a terminus for buses to and from most parts of town.

Two modern buildings farther down on the right are the head offices of the Banks. King Street terminates in a welter of duty free shops at *Harbour Street*. Running parallel to the harbour this street contains the offices of the **Tourist Board**, located in a pink hacienda-like building on its seaward side, and the offices of most of the airlines. The former harbour area to the south, with traditional wooden 'finger piers' alongside which ships could berth within shouting distance of Harbour Street, is being transformed into a modern resort area where only cruise ships

may dock. This will doubtless improve its appearance, but at the expense of its former cheerful albeit somewhat loud and aromatic charm. At the west end of Harbour Street is the **New Victoria Crafts Market**, a large modern centre for the sale of traditional Jamaican straw and wood handcrafts. From the adjacent No 2 Pier a ferry plies across the harbour to Port Royal every hour during early mornings and evenings, and the 50 ft. 'La Carioca' leaves at 10 a.m. daily for a six hour sail round the 'cays' outside the harbour (cost including lunch and a drink is $12). On Saturdays and Sundays 'taxi-trips' to the cays depart 8 a.m., 11 a.m. and 2 p.m. Slightly inland from the Crafts Market, up Pechon Street is the **Railway Station**, departure spot for trains to Montego Bay, Port Antonio, and all towns en route (see timetable on page 33). The streets meeting Harbour Street at right angles from the north each have their in-

37

The eighteenth-century Headquarters House

dividual character. Going from west to east, Orange Street leaves the clubs and bars of its lower reaches, enjoys a brief stretch as West Parade, and later becomes Slipe Road, skirting the teeming warrens of Hannah, Jones and Admiral Towns on its way to Cross Roads. After King and Church Streets comes Duke Street, which has most of the island's insurance head offices in its lower reaches. Farther up on the left hand corner with Beeston Street is **Headquarters House** a striking old eighteenth-century house built by one Thomas Hibbert, as the result of a wager with three other rich Kingston merchants as to who could build the finest house. It has a handsome semi-spiral wooden staircase, and was the seat of Government until 1960 when the legislature removed across the street to the modern **Gordon House**, called after the national hero (see **page 62**). Headquarters House now houses a Government Ministry. Farther up Duke Street, on the corner of Charles Street, is Jamaica's only **Synagogue**, which has in its garden some very old tombstones from a now defunct Jewish cemetery in Kingston. Finally, Duke Street possesses the **Scots (Presbyterian) Kirk**, the present building, with its curious little spire,

also being a replacement for a casualty of the 1907 earthquake. Next comes East Street, which houses, above all, the **Institute of Jamaica**, a large red brick building near to Harbour Street, on the right. It contains the **West India Reference Library**, the greatest collection anywhere of books, articles and prints on the West Indies; an historical museum containing Arawak and Spanish artefacts, relics of slavery, treasures recovered from Port Royal, and a large natural history museum with examples of most types of Jamaican flora and fauna. The Institute has a permanent exhibit of prints, paintings and quotations illustrating West Indian history, and is well worth a visit, preferably as early in your stay as possible. A very unusual exhibit is the **Shark Papers**, the log of the American barque *Nancy* engaged in illicit trade during 1799, when Britain was at war with France, Spain and Holland. When apprehended by a British frigate, the captain threw his very incriminating papers overboard and presented his captors with false ones. Unfortunately for him, by an incredible coincidence the captain of another British warship, one Lieutenant Fitton, while fishing miles away, caught a shark which on being cut open, was found to have the original papers inside it! The *Nancy*'s true business was revealed and the papers were instrumental in convicting her captain and owners. The papers and the jaws of the shark (once labelled 'Lieutenant Fitton recommends these jaws as a collar for neutrals to swear through') can be seen in the Institute's museum. Near to the top end of East Street on the right, the round, modern building is the Tax Department. By the junction of East and North Streets (left) at 11 North Street, is the **Jamaica School of Art**, behind whose attractive main building is a tranquil old-world courtyard flanked by a splendid wooden balconied affair and the former outhouses of the main house. The school has produced some very talented local artists, but no distinctly Jamaican style, as has neighbouring Haiti, for example. The basement of the school houses a small art gallery.

A well preserved example of Jamaican Georgian vernacular architecture can be seen nearby at 90 Hanover Street, a fine old family house (now Government offices) with a beautifully proportioned sweeping front staircase. Also on North Street is the pagodaesque

splendour of the **Chinese Cultural Centre** and, for contrast, farther east is the immense concrete Byzantine dome of the Holy Trinity **Roman Catholic cathedral**. Moving east along Harbour Street we meet *Hanover Street*, formerly Kingston's bar and brothel centre. Both facilities still remain, but are now so run down and disreputable that they derive patronage mainly from sailors whose discrimination has been numbed by rum.

Leaving Parade on the west side is the *Spanish Town Road*, a busy and colourful thoroughfare leading eventually to the former capital. Several hundred yards along on the left is the **Coronation Market**, biggest of Jamaica's markets, a bustling labyrinth of stalls and vendors where virtually anything grown or produced locally can be obtained, if one has time to search for it. The market women (higglers) travel in from the country districts all around Kingston with their produce, Friday and Saturday being the most popular days. Continuing past the over-crowded slums of West Kingston to Three Miles roundabout the Spanish Town Road meets Hagley Park Road on the right leading

The Jamaica School of Art

No. 90 Hanover Street

Simon Bolivar — statue a gift of Venezeula

up past Kingston's new Hindu temple on the left, to *Half Way Tree*. The road on the left at the roundabout is Marcus Garvey Drive, leading through a bleak 300 acre industrial estate, past the busy quays of Newport West where most cargo ships now berth, and eventually back to Harbour Street. Half a mile after the roundabout on the Spanish Town Road a small road left (signposted for Hunt's Bay) leads to the now disused **Jewish Cemetery**. One of the oldest in the New World, it has tombs dating back to 1672. Spanish Town Road, now the A1, carries on through more development, including the large and modern **Red Stripe Brewery**, which can be visited by arrangement, to a junction with Washington Boulevard (right) which leads to *Constant Spring Road* and Half Way Tree. The A1 continues as a dual carriageway to Spanish Town.

Immediately north of Duke and East Street is **King George VI Park** now a shrine, whose

role as Kingston racecourse is commemorated by the former back and home straights being called **East and West Race Course**, respectively. The assortment of large concrete office blocks along East Race Course contain the offices of the Prime Minister and the Ministries of Finance and of Education. The resolute look-ing epauletted gentleman on the pedestal before the Ministry of Education is Simon Bolivar, who spent a seven-month exile in Jamaica, during which time he wrote his Jamaica Letter, one of the key documents of his career, and indeed of South American history. The park contains modern monu-ments to George William Gordon and Paul Bogle, martyrs of the Morant Bay revolt (see page 62), and the tombs of former Prime Minister Sir Donald Sangster and Premier N.W. Manley. Immediately north of the park, on Marescaux Road is an elegant old building with long verandas and a striking clock tower. This is **Mico College** (for teacher training), an institution with interesting origins. In 1670 Lady Mico, widow of a rich London merchant, left £1 000 to a favourite nephew, on condition that he agreed to marry one of her six nieces. After his refusal to do so, the money was invested in land in East London, and the interest devoted to the ransoming of Christians captured by Barbary pirates. By the late eighteenth century piracy in the Mediterranean had been ended and, as the money had multiplied to over £116 000, it was decided in 1835 that Lady Mico would have agreed to its being used to establish schools for the newly-emancipated slaves. The present Mico College is one of these. Marescaux Road leads to the busy inter-section of Cross Roads with its market, shops, cinema and (usually) traffic congestion.

MODERN KINGSTON. The heart of uptown Kingston is a roughly triangular area with the three main roads intersecting at its apices (Cross Roads, Half Way Tree and Matilda's Corner). *Half Way Tree Road*, connecting Cross Roads to Half Way Tree is distinguished mainly by the volume and speed of its traffic. Near its mid-point at the traffic lights beside the large Telephone Company building (left) the road to the right leads to nearby **New Kingston**, a modern development area con-

The restored seventeenth-century Vale Royal

taining the three largest hotels in Kingston (Sheraton, Skyline and Pegasus). The pillared building in its own grounds seen through the trees on the left is the **Liguanea** (pronounced Liganee) **Club** one of the oldest and most respected private clubs in Jamaica. New Kingston is still being developed, but already displays much attractive modern architecture and should be a well designed complement to the many fine old houses surrounding it. It contains banks, insurance offices, restaurants, boutiques and a shopping centre styled on vaguely Spanish lines, numbering among its attractions a very un-Spanish discotheque. New Kingston's north-east boundary is marked by *Trafalgar Road* (with side roads Lord Nelson Way and Hamilton Drive) which, after crossing Hope Road changes battles and continues as *Waterloo Road*. The area north of Trafalgar Road contains many examples of houses built by the richer members of Kingston society after the down-town area became unfashionable. They are spacious and airy, with high tile or cedar shingle roofs,

some with pillared patios, some with verandas, most with wide grounds containing a profusion of flowering shrubs. Perhaps the most beautiful of them is **Vale Royal**, built in 1694 and recently restored and expanded with skill and sensitivity. Traditionally the house of the Deputy Prime Minister, it stands at the sharp bend in Montrose Road off Lady Musgrave Road, which cuts across the east end of Trafalgar Road. It is worth spending a little time driving, or better, walking around the area, to see these glimpses of an older way of life. There is an air of languor and elegance here which is entirely missing from today's housing schemes.

Half Way Tree is a crossroads which derived the second part of its name from a large cotton tree which formerly stood there. No one is sure where it was meant to be half-way between, and it is now graced by a square clock tower bearing a bust of King Edward VII.

To the left, Hagley Park Road goes off to Newport West via Spanish Town Road. Two hundred yards from Half Way Tree on the right it meets *Eastwood Park Road* on the corner of which (left) is *St Andrew Parish Church*, founded in 1692 but now a hotch potch of styles, having been altered and rebuilt many times since. Some interesting monuments have survived and can be seen on the walls inside. Eastwood Park Road (later Red Hills Road) leads to the elevated and expensive suburbs of Red Hills, Stony Hill and Forest Hills, and, via Washington Boulevard which passes over it, left to Spanish Town Road. To the right of Half Way Tree, Hope Road goes northwest to **Matilda's Corner** and **Papine**. After the junction with Trafalgar and Waterloo Roads, it passes (left) the imposing iron entrance gates of **Devon House** built in the nineteenth century by George Stiebel, a Jamaican who, after gold-mining in South America, became perhaps the first negro millionaire in the Caribbean. It is a striking piece of architecture in the classical style, larger and more ambitious than any similar house in Jamaica. Recently restored by the Jamaican National Trust, the house, outbuildings and grounds are a refreshing example of enlightened and tasteful tourism development. The main house is a centre for displays of furnishing, with each room a showcase for a particular period or style, while the former coach-house is now a bar and restaurant, using Old Port Royal as its theme. Meals are served under the shade of the courtyard trees, in sight of the stately Royal Palms and fountain before the main building. To the rear, the former staff quarters, kitchen, harness house, silver vault, etc. have been converted into craft shops, boutiques, and even a museum of African art and history. The meals and drinks served can be recommended both for quality and for their traditional Jamaican character.

Hope Road has several attractive old houses along its length and beyond Devon House on the left is the sentried gate to the residence of the Prime Minister, **Jamaica House**, a white columned building set well back from the road. At the traffic light junction with Lady Musgrave Road (right) and East King's House Road (left, leading to the new housing area of Barbican) is a gate on the first left corner with its personal traffic light. This is the entrance of **King's House**, residence of the Governor-General, set in 200 acres of well tended park. To the left of the main residence is a graceful old wooden building built on brick arches, which houses the secretarial offices. Farther behind, the old stables now serve as garages. The astonishing tree before the house, with huge roots supporting vast horizontal branches and new roots groping their way earthward, is a banyan tree, and it shares with the cotton tree the distinction of being a favourite refuge for 'duppies' (ghosts). Passing back through our individual traffic light, Hope Road continues to *Matilda's Corner* (also called Liguanea) where, at the traffic lights, it joins Old Hope Road, which goes (right) to Cross Roads. Following it, the first road on the left is Munroe Road, leading to Mona Road, and the first on the right off Monroe Road (Beverley Drive) leads up to **Beverley Hills**. Kingston's most exclusive area, built on the formerly undesirable scrub-covered rock of Long Mountain. It is worth driving up to see both the view of Kingston and architectural styles from early Georgian to late King Farouk. Following the road downhill brings us out on to the Old Hope Road shortly before Mountain View Avenue on the left (beside a large Texaco petrol station). This is the direct route to Palisadoes Airport and, a few hundred yards along it (right), is the modern 30 000 capacity **National Stadium**, which housed the 1966 British Commonwealth games. Beside the stadium is the Olympic-size swimming pool and the **National Arena**, used for indoor sport, exhibitions, concerts, etc. Behind the stadium is an aluminium statue of a runner, modelled on Arthur Wint, the great Jamaican runner, who won the quarter-mile gold medal in the 1948 Olympic Games in London.

Leaving Matilda's Corner to the east, Old Hope Road passes between two modern shopping plazas (formerly everyone shopped downtown, but with a recent proliferation of shopping plazas, most shopping is now done locally), and meets Mona Road (right) at Sangster's Book Shop. Mona Road leads past

Devon House

Arthur Wint and the National Stadium

the middle-class housing scheme of Mona Heights (left) and the entrance drive to **Mona Hotel** (right). This was formerly Dunreath Castle, the Great House for Mona sugar estate, one of three estates which occupied most of the plain. It is a well-proportioned, spacious old building and makes a pleasant stop for lunch, dinner or a drink. Mona Road, along which the heavy carts loaded with hogsheads of sugar and puncheons of rum used to roll on their way to the wharves, is now the main approach road to the **University of the West Indies** (U.W.I.), Mona Campus.

UWI, which was founded in 1948 with only thirty-three students and now has 3 500, must be one of the most beautifully situated universities in the world. It is built on the site of the old Mona and Papine sugar estates, ruins of whose mills, storehouses, and aqueducts are scattered among the modern University buildings, mournful reminders of Jamaica's past. The Chapel (right on entering)

is an old sugar factory building from Trelawny, sent stone by stone to UWI and reassembled. Behind it, the remains of the **Mona Sugar Factory**, are well preserved and give us a good idea of how sugar was made in the old days of slavery. A very large 'overshot' wheel (i.e. turned by water fed at the top of the wheel) drove the three great hand-fed rollers which crushed the juice from the cane. This juice flowed along wooden troughs to the adjacent sugar boiling house, the large roofless building, now used as a plant nursery, where it was evaporated to a syrup which crystallised to a mixture of sugar and molasses. The hogshead casks (containing almost a ton) were stored on racks in the eastern part of the building (called the curing house), the molasses dripped out of holes in the bottom, leaving wet brown sugar in the cask. The molasses was then taken to the third building to the south, elegantly constructed and bearing the date '1759' over the main door. This was the 'Still House' where the molasses was fermented and distilled to yield the once famous Mona rum. Not every visitor to the West Indies approved of this praiseworthy practice, for, to quote one in 1651: 'The chief Fudling they make in the Island is Rumbullion, alias Kill-Devil, and this is made of Suggar Canes distilled, a hot hellish and terrible liquor'. The precious fluid was stored in the rum store, a small but very strong building with heavily barred windows, against the southern side of the main building. In 1846 Mona Estate shipped fifty six hogsheads of sugar and thirty two puncheons of rum to England.

Diametrically across Hospital Ring Road from Aqueduct Road is the Hospital Exit to Papine, and a left turn leads to **Papine Market**, one of the smallest but most attractive of Kingston's markets. Its main days are Thursday, Friday and Saturday. Papine marks the north-east boundary of the Corporate Area and a left turn at the road junction takes us down Old Hope Road back to Matilda's Corner. On the right is the entrance to the **College of Arts, Science and Technology** (C.A.S.T.) Jamaica's foremost technical college. Going down Old Hope Road, Mona Heights is now on the left and half a mile down on the right is the entrance to **Hope Botanic Gardens.**

Hope Sugar Estate was the third and largest of the three which formerly occupied the area. The name of the estate and the river flowing through it derive from the first owner, Major Richard Hope, who came to Jamaica with Penn and Venables. The gardens, almost 200 acres of them, contain a very fine Orchid House, with many representatives of Jamaica's 200 native species, a Cactus Garden, a Palm Avenue, ornamental ponds, a little Zoo, a children's fun-fair, and a bandstand where the Jamaica Military Band (dressed as Zouaves, thanks to one of Queen Victoria's brainwaves) play most Sundays. If you want a quiet uncrowded few hours to study the wealth of exotic plant life in the gardens do *not* go at week-ends and particularly never on a Sunday, as half the population of Kingston will be there. It is however an ideal opportunity to see Jamaicans enjoying themselves en masse on their day off. Following the main garden road round to the right just before the funfair and towards the

Mona Aquaduct —
now part of the University of the West Indies

Papine Exit, we come to the plant nursery (left) where ruins of the **Hope Sugar Factory** can be seen. Beyond the exit gate is the magnificent 1758-vintage stone aqueduct which brought water from Hope River to the mill house. Hope Gardens are among the most beautiful in the Caribbean and are well worth two or three hours of anyone's time.

45

PORT ROYAL

PORT ROYAL has been the silent witness to a kaleidoscope of diverse scenes during its turbulent 300 years, from the wild debauches of the buccaneers to their deaths on Gallows Point or Deadman's Cay; from the triumphant return of Morgan from his sack of Panama, to the destruction of the town in the holocaust of 1692; from the tumultuous return of Rodney after victory at the Saints bringing the French flagship as prize, to Benbow's bitter return there to die. More than any other place in Jamaica, Port Royal is where the echoes of her violent past linger most strongly.

Port Royal is situated beyond the airport at the end of the Palisadoes strip, and our route is the reverse of that from the airport to Kingston. Follow Mountain View Avenue south to its termination on Windward Road, then left past Rock Fort to the Harbour View roundabout, and right, along the *Palisadoes strip*. Follow this to the roundabout, where a right turn leads to the airport. We carry on straight ahead for almost 10 miles to Port Royal. The route is one of contrasts, with sea-pounded white beaches on the left, and the finest salt water mangrove swamps in the Caribbean on the right. The sheltering effect of the Palisadoes strip, together with the high level of chemical nutrients inside the harbour account for the luxuriant mangrove growth and its attendant high level of biological activity. Flanked by cactus and mangrove, the road passes the ruin of a large Victorian fort (left); inside are the remains of naval gun sites, magazines, stores and barracks. A mile farther on, the ruin of **Fort Rupert** lies to the left, one of the five forts destroyed in the 1692 earthquake. The fort is now beneath the waters of a sheltered lagoon, but stretches of the walls can be seen a few inches below and, in places, above the surface. Amazingly enough, the ruin was discovered only in 1968 by a member of the Sub Aqua Club who was snorkelling in the lagoon. Behind the high red brick wall on the right of the road was, formerly, the **Naval Dockyard**, a legacy of Port Royal's days as the centre of the West Indies station. After its closure in 1905 the town was reduced to an almost isolated fishing village, approachable only by sea.

Construction of the Palisadoes highway (in 1936) and the siting of the airport nearby have revived the town's fortunes, and the old dockyard now houses a marine and beach club, with the stirringly inaccurate name of **Morgan's Harbour**. This has limited accommodation, restaurant, pool, bar and jetty and is interesting in that some of the old dockyard buildings have been incorporated – for example the present changing rooms used to be the old pitch store in the days when ships required caulking. Adjoining Morgan's Harbour is the **Yacht Harbour**, where many private yachts and motor launches are berthed. It is also a departure point for deep sea game fishing for marlin etc., an exciting, if expensive, sport. At the small square in Port Royal the road right leads down to the fisherman's beach and the landing stage where the ferries from Kingston arrive. The beach, malodorous but primitively picturesque, is a centre for the sale of live lobsters and fresh and fried fish (the latter taste much better than they look; hygiene is not a major consideration in their preparation). Most of the fishing boats are modern versions of dugout canoes, powered by an outboard motor, and it is possible to hire one complete with fisherman for trips out to the beautiful islands (called cays) outside Kingston harbour. Lime Cay is the nearest and largest, **South Cay** the farthest and smallest, but, if you get it to yourself, the most enchanting, being an almost classic desert island. It is advisable to wear a wide-brimmed hat on these trips, as there is no shelter on the boats. Also, sail out early in the morning so that the boat can bring you back before the late afternoon wind rises, otherwise it can be an exciting return trip. There are usually a few frigate birds and pelicans hovering around offshire, with the latter occasionally dropping like a stone into the water after fish. At the far end of the beach, the Jamaica National Trust has built a large wooden outlook tower which affords a view over beach and town. The big iron-framed building with pillars and open balconies beyond the tower is the **Old**

Landing stage in Port Royal

Naval Hospital built in 1819, in the period when mortality from fever was frightful. It is being renovated as a museum for artifacts recovered from Port Royal, and will also house a lecture-theatre and archaelogical laboratories. Port Royal's destruction provided a unique opportunity to study the day-to-day life of 1692, petrified in mid stride as it were. The first shock of the earthquake sent half the city into the sea, and much of the rest was buried, yielding almost a latter-day Pompeii. Most items of value were removed by looters and divers as soon as it was safe to do so, but recent archaelogical finds include cannon, pewter and silver ware, ceramic jars, bottles and plates, and a hoard of silver pieces of eight from the Royal mints at Lima in Peru, and Potosi in Bolivia. The most touching item recovered is a brass watch whose hands stopped at 11.39 – the time the earthquake struck! Most of the recovered items are in the Institute of Jamaica.

47

Eyes right! Police parade (see opposite page)

Passing across the town square we come to the **Parish Church of St Peter's**, on the far left corner. The lady caretaker, who lives just opposite, will usually open the church for visitors, and will insist on showing some items of silver plate reputed to have belonged to Henry Morgan and to have been taken by him from the cathedral in Panama. Among the items is a two-pint tankard from which he is

alleged to have drunk, using the whistle on the bottom of the handle to summon a refill! The story is in keeping with Morgan's bibulous habits, but there is little evidence that the items were ever his. The original brickwork of the church has been covered on the outside by an unfortunate cement rendering, but the interior is charmingly simple. The memorial tablets on the walls are a chilling reminder of just how terrible a toll yellow fever took of Europeans in the tropics. The wooden organ gallery is noteworthy for the fine carvings, the work of local craftsmen during the age of slavery, and the graceful brass candelabrum dates from 1743. Prominent among the graves in the ill-kept church-yard is that of **Lewis Galdy**, the Frenchman who was swallowed and regurgitated by successive shocks during the 1692 earthquake. As can be seen by a plaque just inside the church door (right) Galdy was instrumental in having the church built, and was one of its first wardens.

After St Peter's, the road passes through the gate of the **Police Training Depot** (visitors are expected to sign the visitors' book), then past the restored arch of a gate from the old boundary wall, along the edge of the large sea-fringed parade ground to the entrance to **Fort Charles**, which alone of Port Royal's six original forts has withstood earthquake, fire and hurricane, and is remarkably well preserved. Founded in 1656 the fort was strengthened by Morgan, further expanded in the 1700s and, at the height of its powers, boasted over 100 cannon, which covered land and sea approaches. Due to both earthquake and shore movements the fort is now well inland, but it was formerly on the water's edge. The main gate, flanked by two huge ship's anchors of the type used by men-of-war in Nelson's day, is guarded by many of the original cannon. The fortress interior is a large walled enclosure on two levels, with raised wooden platforms running along the south and west walls. The two-storied houses in the centre were probably living quarters for the commander and officers while the single storey building on the east side was a munitions store. The buildings have been discreetly renovated as a museum (the candelabra are replicas of the one in St Peter's church). The wooden walkway to the right of the gate inside the western parapet is known as *Nelson's Quarterdeck*, as it was from here during his few weeks as Commander of Fort Charles in 1779 that he kept watch for the anticipated French invasion fleet. The wall of the battery carries a simple plaque stating 'In this place dwelt Horatio Nelson, you who tread his footprints remember his glory'. On the outside of the battery wall are three crosses which locals attribute to 'Nelson's three wives'; a more likely explanation is that they were a memorial to now forgotten fever victims.

Beyond the fort to the south are the ruins of the **Victoria and Albert Batteries** consisting originally of four large naval gun emplacements interconnected by tunnels and underground magazines. The battery was destroyed by the 1907 earthquake and one of the great gun barrels, remarkably unrusted, still lies beside its crazily-angled circular mounting pit. Another distorted reminder of nature's power is the **Giddy House**, formerly the Royal Artillery storehouse, whose angle has a disturbing effect on the inner ear, making an attempt to walk across the sloping floor an unnerving experience.

Giddy House today

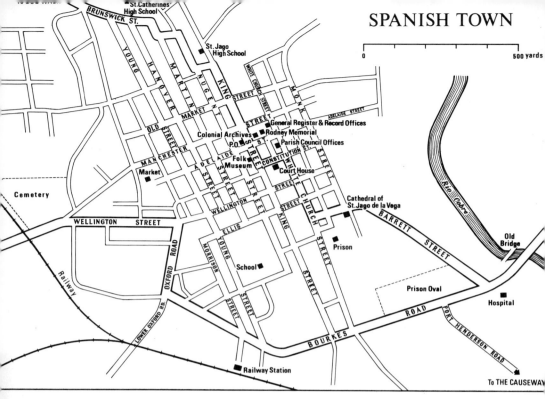

SPANISH TOWN

SPANISH TOWN. The Spanish capital of **Villa de la Vega** (The Town on the Plain) was founded in 1523. During the sack of the town by Cromwell's troops in 1655, all evidences of Papism were destroyed. These included two monasteries, an abbey and two churches, and the work was done with such thoroughness that there is today no trace of anything Spanish in Spanish Town, apart from the homage of street names such as *Red Church* and *WhiteChurch Streets* (after the chapels of the Red Cross and the White Cross) and *Monk Street* (after the Franciscan and Dominican monks). The Anglican Cathedral was built on the site of the Chapel of the Red Cross. English **St Jago de la Vega** (adopting, strangely, the Spaniards' patron saint of the island, which they called Santiago) followed the existing pattern of gridiron streets around the central Plaza Mayor which contained the abbey, the *cabildo* or Town Hall, and the Hall of the Audiencia. This plaza was developed by the English into a square which was without equal in the West Indies. The focal point of Jamaica's society life was King's House, the residence of the Governor-General, representing the monarch. This was completed in 1765, at a cost of £30 000. The historian Edward Long said of it: 'It is now thought to be the noblest and best edifice of its kind, either in North America or any of the British Colonies in the West Indies'. Through King's House for over 100 years trooped a succession of famous visitors. The sailors Nelson, Rodney, Bligh and King William IV (as a princely ensign), naturalists Philip Gosse and Sir Hans Sloane, historian Edward Long, and a succession of Jamaica's governors. Among the latter was John Eyre, who refused to come out of King's House to hear the grievances of black peasants led by Paul Bogle who had walked over sixty miles to see him. Had he listened he might have averted the Morant Bay rebellion (see page 62) and the loss of so many lives. From the steps of King's House in 1838, Governor Sir Lionel Smith proclaimed the abolition of slavery. Emancipation split the plantocratic foundations of Spanish Town's power. The great

50

days ended in 1872 when the seat of government was transferred to Kingston. The hundred years since this transfer have seen the decline of Spanish Town, but the beauty and interest of the old square and surrounding area remain, and make a visit to St Jago de la Vega an essential part of any visit to Jamaica.

ROUTE

Spanish Town is 14 miles along the A1 west of Kingston. From Half Way Tree take the first left (Molynes Road) after St Andrew's Parish Church. This passes through an undistinguished part of town to reach Washington Boulevard where a left turn leads past shopping plazas and modern churches to meet the A1 at Spanish Town Road. A mile to the west of the junction we pass **Ferry Inn** (right) formerly the half-way staging post between Spanish Town and Kingston in the days of horse travel. In 1677 a toll ferry (rider plus horse fifteen pence, sheep and pigs sixpence each) was established across the river, and an Inn built. The lower floor of the present inn is still largely the original stonework. At the junction with a minor road 3 miles beyond the inn, the right-hand road leads through cane fields to the **Caymanas Country Club** and its first-class golf course. The area derives its name from the crocodiles (caimans) which inhabited it in former swampy days. The road on the left of the A1 leads to Port Henderson via the **Caymanas Race Track**, scene of horse-racing on Wednesdays and Saturdays from 12 – 5 p.m.. Continuing through Central Village, the A1 meets the A2 (straight ahead to Old Harbour and the west) on the outskirts of Spanish Town. Our route follows the A1 (right) along Barrett Street (eventually) to the North Coast. Passing the forbidding looking prison on the left, we come (left) to **Spanish Town Cathedral** (the Cathedral Church of St James) which Jamaicans like to claim as the oldest cathedral in any of the former British Colonies. The claim is only strictly true of the foundations, as the present building, founded in 1714, to replace the 1666 building (destroyed by hurricane in 1712) is the third church on the site. The cathedral is, nonetheless, historically the most interesting building certainly in Spanish Town and probably in Jamaica. Built in the form of a cross, and predominantly of brick, it shows two architectural styles, the older part Romanesque and the later additions Gothic. The brick

tower with its quaint little two-stage wooden steeple, was added in 1831. The tombs in and around the cathedral are almost a chronicle of the notables in Jamaica's history. The black and white marble flagstones in the aisles are interspersed with tombstones, and the walls are heavy with marble memorials. The communion plate contains a flagon dating from 1685. three complete six-piece sets, and a chalice bearing the rather touching inscription 'Purchased for Golden Grove Chapel by the slaves on the estate, 1830'.

After the cathedral Barrett Street meets White Church Street, where we turn right, and, after two blocks, reach Constitution

King's House, Spanish Town

Cathedral Church of St. James

The Rodney Memorial

Street and the **Old Town Square**, which we enter at the south-west corner. The Square centrepiece is a picturesque and graceful little park, whose fountain and cannon are dominated by the towering Royal Palms. Each side of the square consists of one building. The stately pillared facade on the west side is **King's House**, or what remains of it, as the building fell into disrepair after the transfer of Government to Kingston, and was gutted by fire in 1925. Plans to restore it for use as a national museum are hindered by the unfortunate and strange fact that there exist no plans, drawings or photographs of it as it was. A model to be seen in the neighbouring Folk Museum is based on written description,

excavation, and one painting of doubtful veracity. Excavations have yielded artifacts going back to Spanish times and it seems that King's House occupies at least in part, the site of the Spanish Hall of Audience. A museum of artifacts has been established on the site. The stables to the left of the facade escaped the 1925 fire, and now house the **Jamaican Folk Museum**, a modest collection of items from Jamaican life through the years, from furniture to a fire engine, including a village store. On the north side of King's House is the **Rodney Memorial**, commemorating his victory of 1782 over the French Fleet under deGrasse in the Battle of the Saints. This saved Jamaica from French

52

invasion, and a statue of Rodney was commissioned by a duly grateful Assembly. On the pedestal are three interesting bas-reliefs, one of which shows the French flagship *Ville de Paris* striking her colours in surrender. The two beautifully worked cannon which flank the statue *Le Modeste* and *Le precipice* came from the flagship and were cast in the Royal Foundry at Douay in 1748. The temple structure over the statue was an afterthought, as were the two terminal buildings. That on the left, the Old Armoury, now houses part of the National Archives and the one on the right is the Registry.

Facing Rodney across the park, on the south side, is the **Court House**, the most recent of the four buildings, being built in 1819. The court occupies the ground floor, and, when in session, fills the pavement and road outside with an animated throng of pursuants, defendants, witnesses and spectators. The upstairs floor contains the **Town Hall**, used for concerts, plays, etc. The remaining building, occupying the east side of the square, is the old **House of Assembly**. Built in 1762, it is easily the most attractive building on the square, with the superb brickwork of its shady colonnade running the entire length of the ground floor, and a secluded wooden pillared balcony above. Formerly the meeting place of Jamaica's governing body, the House was the scene of bitter and stormy debates during the perpetual disputes between the Assembly and successive Governors. The ground floor houses the Parish Library, upstairs are the Parish Council offices, Council Chamber, and Mayor's Parlour, reached by the centrally situated main staircase.

The streets around the Old Town Square contain numbers of admirable old town houses, many of which, unfortunately, have been allowed to fall into disrepair, while others have been restored, not always too happily. The original buildings had fine brickwork, shingled roofs, and wooden louvred windows, including the projecting type known locally as 'coolers'. Modern repairs unfortunately include painting over the brick, replacing shingles with corrugated iron, and installing aluminium or glass louvres. Many examples of these can be seen, but also some well preserved old houses, particularly in

The House of Assembly

White Church, Red Church, King, Wellington and *Nugent streets*. A stately example of an old town house is **Altersheim House** on King Street. Note the portico, brickwork, and 'cooler' windows. Other impressive buildings are the well-proportioned eighteenth-century **Barracks**, occupying the block between Nugent Street and Young Street and the **Baptist Church** on the corner of William and French Streets. This is also called *Phillippo's Church* because of its connection with the pioneer missionary and emancipationist who built it by public subscription. It was opened in 1827 and the collection on the first day, almost entirely from slaves, was over £84.

53

The rugged grandeur of the Blue Mountain Range extends from Kingston's northern suburbs over to the north coast. The area encompasses some of the most beautiful scenery in the island, perhaps in the world. It includes the highest mountain on the island (Blue Mountain Peak 7 402 ft.), a spectacularly sited botanic garden (Cinchona, between 4 500 and 5 500 ft.), a beautiful National Park and bird sanctuary (Hardwar Gap) plus old plantations, great houses, and, for the energetic, some magnificent hill walks. To do justice to the area, at least three days are necessary and the best plan is to establish a central base at, say, *Pine Grove Hotel* and make expeditions from there. As everyone may not have sufficient time to allow for this, the main route is given as a one-day excursion from Kingston, and three supplementary digressions from the main route are recommended, each of which is, in itself, a one day expedition from Kingston. All are very worthwhile and should be experienced if at all possible. Not all the roads are paved, and a sturdy, preferably compact vehicle is advisable. A Volkswagen is perfectly suitable. The roads from Kingston to Mavis Bank via Guava Ridge and Kingston to Section via Hardwar Gap are paved and passable in all weathers, but the road between Guava Ridge and Section is unpaved, and can be difficult during or immediately after heavy rains, as is true of the road after Mavis Bank to Blue Mountain Peak.

Some comments which may be helpful:

The only **petrol station** on the route is at Papine, and it is a good idea to check petrol and tyre pressure there. The road has many bends and while it is generally little used, stay well over on your own side and sound your horn before each bend.

The two small **hotels** on the route, Pine Grove and Bamboo Lodge, have a spectacular view, and a bar.

Carry a **sweater** or jacket for wear in the evening, as it can get quite chilly up at 4 000 feet, and wear stout shoes, as the area is ideal for walking, being cool, beautiful and criss-crossed with inviting paths and tracks.

Bus Services. From Papine, return bus services operate every hour or half hour to Irish Town, to Gordon Town, and to Mavis Bank. There is also a daily local bus to Hagley Gap, depart Papine at around 4 p.m. – depart Hagley Gap at 6 a.m.

MAIN ROUTE: Kingston, Guava Ridge, Hardwar Gap, Newcastle, Kingston

The B1 follows Hope Road from Half Way Tree to Papine. At Papine it passes either right or left round the little park and continuing as the Gordon Town Road, follows the valley of the Hope River, crossing the river by a narrow bridge just before *Blue Mountain Inn* (an exclusive and not cheap establishment). About a hundred yards further on at **Cooperage** the B1 forks left to Newcastle via Irish Town, while our road lies straight ahead to Guava Ridge via Gordon Town. At this junction, a smaller unpaved road, on the right just beyond the bus stop leads down to the river, and to **Dunsinane Pen**, an old coffee plantation. The front staircase to the great house can still be seen, from which the proclamation of the

Abolition of Slavery was read to the local slaves in 1838, also the ruins of some of the old buildings. The coffee produced was shipped in wooden casks, made across the way at the Cooperage by imported Irish coopers, who were quartered farther up the Mamee River road at the village still called **Irish Town.**

A few hundred yards farther along, the route passes through a village called Industry, a slightly incongruous name in view of the normal level of activity there. Three miles from Papine, 1 200 ft. up in the valley of the Hope River, stands **Gordon Town**, a metropolis by Blue Mountain standards, possessing a police station, a court-house (typical local crimes 'cussin bad words' and 'stone throwing'), a post office, two schools, and a convent. Gordon Town was the site of Jamaica's first botanic garden, established by

View from Guava Ridge

Hinton East in 1770 at Spring Garden. East introduced hundreds of foreign plant species from places as diverse as China and Sweden. Many of his imports, such as Hibiscus, Azalea, Cassia, Magnolia, Oleander, Croton and Jasmine flourished, and permanently altered the Jamaican scene. Nothing survives of the original garden although the town has a profusion of attractive plant life on all sides. Gordon Town is connected to Newcastle, Irish Town, Content Gap and Flamstead by a series of footpaths radiating along the valleys and ridges which converge on the town. The tracks are well defined and although fairly steady climbs (the steepest, that to Newcastle, rises 2 300 ft. in 3 miles) are well within the capabilities of the average walker.

The road to **Guava Ridge** leaves the town square on the right by the police station, crosses the Hope River by a narrow bridge and climbs above the town along the side of the river valley. As the road twists and turns in and out of a succession of valleys, the red roofs of Newcastle constantly appear and recede from view, 4 000 ft. up across the valley, straggling down the mountainside, and looking, especially in low cloud, like some lost Inca city in the Andes. A succession of tiny houses are dotted along the route, some clinging precariously to the hillside, each the centre of a small patch of banana, coffee, vegetables, etc. Down below the road, many more can be seen scattered over the valley floor. Such small-holdings supply the majority of Kingston's vegetables and fruit and, as the week-end approaches the road is busy with brightly painted market trucks carrying unbelievable loads of higglers (women vendors) with their baskets of produce to the various city markets. This was the free land settled by the newly emancipated slaves in 1834, and the pattern of their agricultural life has not changed significantly since then. Two hairpin bends straddle the eleven-mile post as the road climbs steadily around the sides of the mountains. Shortly before the fourteen-mile post a broad dirt road on the right leads to **Galloway Lodge**, an old Great House sited among pine and pimento trees, with a wonderful panoramic view. With care, the road is drivable up to the house, and continues beyond it as a very scenic footpath leading to **Flamstead** 2 miles away. The first road junction is beside a bus

55

shelter immediately before Guava Ridge at an elevation of 3 000 ft. The righthand road passes through the scattered township of Guava Ridge and descends via **Mavis Bank** to the *Yallahs River* at 1 700 ft. Our route is the ascending road on the left which is paved for a further mile or so then becomes a good dirt road. Shortly before this, on the right, is the entrance drive leading up to *Pine Grove Hotel*, a pleasantly ramshackle old building with a commanding view of a distant Kingston and truly a Jamaican hotel in that most of its patrons are locals. One of the most rewarding Jamaican experiences is to sit on the verandah here in the evening with mountains all around, while the sky changes from blue through turquoise to pink, and the lights of the capital gradually come to life far below. Flowers grow profusely around the hotel, which operates Pine Grove Florist Shop at Mona. After Pine Grove, the road passes **Valda** (3 758 ft.) on the left, then drops steadily, with a fine view to the north-east along the valley, to **Content Gap**, a village connected by footpath to Gordon Town, 4 miles and 1 800 ft. below. At the round water tank the left-hand track offers an easy one-mile walk up to **Charlottenburg House**, an uninhabited but well preserved Great House, furnished with antique Jamaican furniture. The former slave quarters, dating from coffee plantation days, still stand adjacent to the house. The durable and attractive hardwood used in the construction is local cedar, cut from the plantation when it was cleared for coffee. Continuing along the main road, shortly after **St Peters**, there is a junction with the road to **Clydesdale**, a very picturesque forestry station sited on the river Clyde about one mile up a rather bumpy little road. This also was once a coffee plantation and retains coffee-drying barbecues and an old water wheel as legacies of the period. It is an ideal centre for hill walking, being the focal point of many forestry tracks, and is within easy walking (or driving) distance from **Cinchona**. The Forestry Department rents the two-bedroomed main house at Clydesdale for a nominal amount ($5 per day, linen, towels etc. not provided). On the way up to Clydesdale, the little road passes **Chestervale Youth Camp**, where youngsters from Kingston get an opportunity to escape from the heat and social pressures of that city for a few months while learning the basis of some trade. Back on the main route, half a mile after the Clydesdale detour, a small road on the right leads to **Silver Hill** coffee factory where, between September and February, it is possible to see the red coffee berries having the outer pulp removed from the two inner green beans, ready for drying, husking, and roasting. In the Blue Mountains optimum soil and climatic conditions combine to produce a coffee of exceptionally fine flavour, which is the most expensive and sought after in the world. After the introduction of coffee in 1728, its cultivation spread through the Blue Mountains, and most of the Great Houses here were plantation houses built during the halcyon years 1800 to 1840, when coffee exports rose to 17 000 tons per year. After emancipation the large plantations declined, and were split up between small farmers, instituting a system which has never produced more than a fraction of the earlier tonnages. Silver Hill, owned by the Jamaica Agricultural Society, is one of three coffee factories in the Blue Mountains.

At **Section** the road joins the B1 which connects Kingston to the North Coast at Buff Bay. The right-hand partially paved road runs north through the mountains via villages with such engaging names as *Birnamwood* and *Tranquility*, to Buff Bay. Our route to the left is, at **Hardwar Gap** (4 000 ft.), the highest paved road in Jamaica. The hills around the Gap constitute **Hollywell Forest Park**, a fine example of montane mist forest. The area has an annual rainfall of over 100 inches a year, with wet clinging mists being an almost daily occurrence. Under the influence of this almost constant moisture, the flora is quite distinct even from that of Newcastle only 2 miles away. Pine trees predominate among the many tree types, while a striking feature is the profusion of a wide selection of Jamaica's 550 types of fern, including the high tree ferns (*Cyathea arborea*). Some of the trees grow to over 30 ft., and many support epiphytes, climbing plants and even orchids. The bird song which fills the forest normally includes the harsh cry of the red-headed *Jamaican Woodpecker* and the hauntingly plaintive call of the *Solitaire Thrush*. Picnic rondavels with views of Kingston are dotted over the hillside, and the Forestry Department rents a few attractive log cabins at very reasonable rates (as for Clydesdale, also two-bed cabins for $4).

From Hardwar Gap the B1 continues towards Newcastle, following the contours of **Mount Horeb**, with views over the Mammee river valley.

Newcastle is a military camp built between 3 500 and 4 000 ft. up on the mountainside. The main road (B1) passes straight over the parade ground. The camp was established in 1841 by General Sir William Gomm, at that time in command of British troops, in an attempt to reduce the fearfully high death rate from yellow fever. The success of building a hill station above the fever line was shown immediately, as there were no fever cases among 130 troops of the newly arrived King's Royal Rifle Corps who were sent there, whereas a quarter of their 400 colleagues down on the plain died within two months. For over 100 years the camp was the depot of a succession of British regiments, some of which left their regimental crests on the high wall behind the cannon on the north side of the parade ground. A new crest is the crocodile of the Jamaica Defence Force, whose regimental depot Newcastle now is. Visitors may use the bar and facilities of the Sergeant's mess, located in the building above the parade ground, and the army also rents out a series of comfortable cottages a mile above the camp. The mountain looming above Newcastle is **Catherine's Peak** (5 056 ft.), named after the first woman known to have climbed it, the sister of the historian Edward Long. It is an easy one hour each way climb from the parade ground.

From Newcastle the road drops steadily to the few houses which constitute **Irish Town**, passing the signposted entrance drive up to *Strawberry Hill Hotel* on the right just before entering. This attractive old house, surrounded by lawns, gardens and woods, is sited on a hilltop with a panoramic view which includes Kingston. After Irish Town the road winds past a road on the right leading to the small hotel Bamboo Lodge, then *Belancita*, home of Sir Alexander Bustamente, and down the mountainside to meet the Mammee River, whose course it then follows down to the Blue

Mavis Bank (see opposite)

Mountain Inn at Cooperage junction, and right for Kingston.

Flamstead

Approaching Guava Ridge Road junction from Kingston the Mavis Bank road (right) descends around a bend. Immediately after this bend, a smaller road goes steeply up to the right. This is our route to **Flamstead**. Half a mile up where the road forks, we take the left-hand-descending road. Henceforth, at other junctions with smaller roads, we follow the larger ascending road, rising through the eucalyptus forest. Immediately beyond the point when eucalyptus gives way to Caribbean pine is a T-junction with a broad road where we turn right. The left-hand road leads to a dramatic saddle between two valleys called **Governor's Bench**, after Sir Alexander Swettenham, Governor of the Island during the earthquake of 1907 which largely destroyed Kingston. After a few hundred yards our route to the right passes (left) **Bellevue Great House**, a rambling structure built around 1793 by a French refugee from the bloody slave revolution in neighbouring Haiti. Now owned by the University of the West Indies and run as a guest house for staff and visitors, it has a magnificent setting amid the mountains, with a view over

57

Newcastle high in the mountains

Kingston Harbour. Our way continues past a small road (right) leading to *Nomdimi*, a modest cottage set among pine trees, home of the late Norman Manley and his artist wife Edna, and still used by Mrs. Manley. Continuing past views over the valley to the Governor's Bench and Mount Rosanna to the south, we meet a narrow road (right) which leads eventually as a footpath to **Galloway Lodge** great house. The path, mainly level and easily negotiable, includes memorable views down a variety of valleys. Immediately after this road comes a broad dirt road (right) which leads, also as a footpath, initially along the saddles between deep river valleys, then down into the valley of the Salt River to Gordon Town. Our road straight ahead meets the rough ascending drive up to **Flamstead House**. The road continues (left) by Content and Dallas down the valleys of the Barbecue and Cane Rivers, eventually meeting the main south coast road at Bull Bay.

Flamstead is at present a semi-derelict jumble of buildings, old and not so old. The original Great House was visited by Nelson and later owned by Governor Eyre, who was in residence there when news of the Morant Bay revolt was brought to him. After its destruction in the 1907 earthquake, the present structure was erected and enjoyed a period as a hotel, but inaccessibility and neglect have combined to reduce it to its present sad state of peeling paint and cobwebbed four posters glimpsed through dim panes. To the rear of the main building stands (but only just) the remnant of a small summer house, which commands possibly the finest view in Jamaica. Flamstead is sited on a forward ridge of the Blue Mountains and has an unrestricted view of Kingston, Port Royal, the harbour and the entire Liguanea Plain. There is also a panoramic sweep of the grand ridge of the Blue Mountains as background, and Dallas and Long Mountain in the foreground, between the house and the sea. The large expanse of water on the Flamstead side of Long Mountain is **Mona Reservoir** with the campus of UWI beside it. Far above the noise and smell of traffic and people, with only the ever-present John Crows circling the valleys below, here is tranquility indeed.

In the field adjacent to the house (right on entering) there is, incredibly, at nearly 400 ft., a shipwreck! During Flamstead's period as a hotel, the field in question housed a phenomenon called a *seven year pond*, this being a body of water which appeared and disappeared for alternate seven (roughly) year periods. The hotel owner had the bright idea of dragging a boat up the mountain and launching it as a floating bar, moored on the magic mere. An unintentional blow for temperance was struck by the Forestry Department, who by large scale local planting of eucalyptus, which require a lot of water, lowered the water table, causing the pond to disappear, and the buoyant boozer to founder.

CINCHONA

These botanic gardens cling to a magnificent stretch of ridge which plummets from 5 500 to 4 500 ft. high above the valleys of the Yallahs, Clyde and Green Rivers. Cinchona has certainly the most inspiring site of any botanic garden in Jamaica, and most probably in the world. It was founded in 1868 as a centre for the cultivation of Assam tea and cinchona trees, whose bark was in great demand as a source of quinine for the treatment of malaria. The cinchona is a native of the high Andes, and its medicinal properties had been learnt by the Spaniards from the Quechua descendants of the Incas. An experimental few hundred acres were planted around Cinchona and proved initially profitable. Later, however, production on a bigger scale in India was cheaper, and the Jamaican plantations of both cinchona and tea failed. The plantation shrank to an expatriate's dream, a 'European Garden'. This was established by an English gardener to supply Kingston with flowers and vegetables and as a result of its success production of these items is now an important source of income for local people.

Cinchona affords views in all directions, with John Crow Peak and St John's Peak to the north; the main ridge of the Blue Mountains stretching east and viewed spectacularly from the **Panorama Walk** on the east side of the gardens, and Kingston and the sea shimmering away to the hot south. The gardens are shaped rather like a longish triangle with its base at the top (north) and the apex at the bottom (south). The ridge runs from 5 500 ft. in the north to 4 500 in the south and the main points of interest are sited in the lower half below the **Great House** which was formerly the home of Jamaica's Superintendent of Gardens. It is now uninhabited but furnished, and may be rented by the day from the present superintendent at Hope Gardens, Kingston. This is the ideal way to see Cinchona, but be sure to take sweaters, jackets and stout shoes in addition to food and drink. Before the house are well tended lawns bordered by a profusion of flowers; around the lawns is a virtual labyrinth of paths and walks leading through the loosely arranged trees. These include many imported types, among them some huge specimens of Eucalyptus, easily recognisable by their spear shaped leaves and peeling whitish barks; Juniper; Cork Oak, whose bark is in fact cork; Chinese Cypress; ferns and tree ferns; Rubber Trees, whose leaves when plucked emit a white latex; and some fine examples of Blue Mountain Yacca, a tall tree with tiny dagger-shaped leaves and reddish marks on its smooth trunk. Your enjoyment and knowledge will be greatly increased by enlisting the services of Mr. Clough, the head gardener, who lives in a house near the south end of the garden. He is a very helpful and knowledgeable man. Details and maps of the garden are also given in Alan Eyre's little book (see bibliography page 3).

ROUTE

There are two ways to get there, and three ways to leave.
a) Drive via Clydesdale 1½ miles to **Top Mountain** (dirt road but drivable) then take the signposted jeep road to the left. This is steep and rough but a Volkswagen or similar tough, high-clearance car will make it. Follow the main track to the right of all junctions and you will enter the garden in the middle of the west side. You can of course, park the car at Top Mountain and walk up the jeep road. It climbs 1 000 ft. in its 2 miles, and so is quite strenuous (but it is also very scenic). If walking, try the northern entrance via **St Helen's Gap**, reached so; turn right at a junction beside a water tank and a field of flowers; a couple of hundred yards later there is another intersection. The road ahead leads to a junction with three other broad tracks at St Helen's Gap. The right hand one leads down through a shady pine-avenue to the lawns in front of the Great House. This is the most attractive entrance to the garden.

59

b) If your car is not tough and high, and you would rather drive 5 bumpy miles than climb one, then, at Top Hill continue past the jeep road for 5 miles to **Westphalia**, and park beside the water tank there. It is then a one mile walk up the bridle path (keep left) to the southern (lower) end of the garden.

c) If your car is very tough and high, and you are too, you might consider the direct route from Cinchona, down one of the most diabolical roads in the history of communications.

Called **Slippery Down**, it is unpaved, rough, tortuous; it drops over one and a half thousand feet in less than a mile – an average gradient of one in three. After Westphalia comes **Hall's Delight**, where we take the left road at the T-junction, and emerge with smoking brakes 1 500 ft. lower at a flat bridge crossing Yallahs River. The road on the other side climbs to Mavis Bank, where a right turn takes us through the town and up to Guava Ridge.

Blue Mountain Peak

This, at 7 402 ft. the highest point in Jamaica, is accessible only to such hardy types as are prepared to scramble for three hours or more up a rough track, and the greatest reward falls to those who are prepared to do it in the dark. The view from the peak is, needless to say, breathtaking, unless conditions are misty, in which case it is non-existent. The probability of clear weather is greatest in the early morning so that, with the additional advantage of experiencing the beauty of dawn over the mountains, the effort and inconvenience of beginning the ascent at 2 a.m. are worthwhile. It is possible to drive as far as **Whitfield Hall** a hostel 5 miles from and 3 200 ft. lower than the peak. From here the average gradient is one in nine, and although some parts are much steeper than this, it is no more than a hill walk along a well defined path, and is certainly not mountain climbing.

The vegetation type changes as we climb, from montane mist forest around Whitfield Hall through to the so-called *Elfin Woodland* which starts at around 5 500 ft. and peters out in windswept scrub on the summit. The montane mist forest, which constitutes some of the rare remnants of Jamaica's original forest, derives its characteristics from the mist which often lies on the peaks between 10 am. and 4 pm. This reduces the incident sunlight greatly, thus affecting the flora as described in the case of Hardwar Gap (p. 56). Elfin Woodland is open woodland of mainly short, twisted, gnarled trees, often laden with lichens, epiphytes, mosses and ferns. The greenish grey moss which festoons most trees combines with the usually swirling mist to give the landscape an eerie aspect. This is accentuated by the dwarf trees, many of which are shrunken versions of tall trees at lower altitude, and many dwarf species of orchid, such as the tiny *Lepanthes*, are to be found. Other flowers which grow well are Honeysuckle, Rhododendron, Ginger Lilies, and the lesser-known but irridescently beautiful *Merianias* (called 'Jamaica Rose') whose red, hanging rose-like flowers appear, when sunlight strikes them, to be lit from within.

ROUTE

From Guava Ridge the road descends through pine woods along the broad valley of the Fall River to **Mavis Bank**. After one of the many bends there suddenly unfolds a panoramic view of a section of the Grand Ridge, including Blue Mountain Peak, which is not a sharp, discrete cone in the Matterhorn style, but a rather rounded hump amid a series of others almost equally high. The view down the valley and across the wide Yallahs valley is superb. Shortly before Mavis Bank, at a point where the main road bears left over a bridge, the dirt road which carries straight ahead leads into the local **Central Coffee Factory** where the preparation and roasting of Blue Mountain Coffee beans may be seen. The main road passes above the little factory and affords a good view of it. Mavis Bank is a small township boasting nevertheless both a police station and a post office. The main and only street runs downhill through the town, and terminates in a fork, the left branch of which leads down to the Yallahs River crossing at *Slippery Down*. We take the right fork, along a descending road which soon degenerates to a broad dirt track (easily drivable). It picks its way between groups of little houses and across a narrow bridge over the Falls River, and finally drops sharply to the Yallahs River at **Mahogany Vale**. Our route is down the steep river bank and straight (if possible) through the Yallahs River. This is not possible when the river is high after rains but in normal circumstances, most cars (except minis, etc., with tiny wheels) will make it. If you are heavily laden, the passengers should walk across the adjacent footbridge. Those who make the far bank will find a rough dirt road which climbs steeply to **Hagley Gap**, the nearest village to the Peak. Here at the tiny square in front of the village store, we take the dirt road going up to the left. The other road descends via Cedar Valley to St Thomas and the east. After climbing for one mile to Farm Hill we bear right (the road ahead leads to Penlyne Castle) and continue climbing for half a mile or so to **Whitfield Hall** on the left. Drive in and park before the house. It is clean and homely, if somewhat ascetic, and resembles a European Youth Hostel. It is run by a charming old Englishman, Mr. Algrove, aided by his son John at week-ends. Cooking and washing facilities are provided, as are blankets, and cold drinks are available. You must, however, provide your own food and linen. The house is quaint, the surrounding countryside is ultra-scenic, and there is unlimited scope for hill-walking even for those who have no desire to tackle the Peak.

For those who do, the road from the house leads up past **Abbey Green**, an old coffee factory, and then narrows to a footpath for the remainder of the climb. If you intend doing the night-hike, it is a good plan to carry a flashlight, although paraffin lanterns are available at Whitfield Hall. The house is seldom full, but it is popular at week-ends, especially with youngsters, so lovers of peace and quiet are advised to make the trip during the week.

Cloud over Hagley Gap

This is one of the most diversely attractive parts of the island, being mountainous and, on account of its high rainfall, Jamaica's most lushly tropical region. In spite of its scenic beauty and a profusion of white beaches, it is comparatively neglected by tourists. The route is roughly horseshoe-shaped, following the coast around the Blue Mountains and the adjacent John Crow Mountains, a little explored towering limestone wilderness. Included in the route are Morant Bay, famous for the rebellion of 1865; Bath, mineral water spa and site of an eighteenth-century Botanic Garden, Frenchman's Cove, reputedly the most expensive hotel in the world, and Port Antonio, enjoying the most exquisite setting of all Jamaican towns. Added to these are a scattering of beaches, ruins, great houses, forts and plantations, all with vistas of distant mountains looming behind. Several good hotels are located in and around Port Antonio, and to do justice to the area, at least one overnight stop is advisable.

ROUTE

The road from Kingston to the Airport is followed until the Harbour View roundabout, where, instead of turning right along the Palisadoes strip, we carry straight ahead along the A4 towards **Yallahs**. After some second-rate grey sand beaches enjoying rhapsodic names such as *Copacabana* and *Wickie Wackie*, comes **Bull Bay** where the road (left) leads 7 miles up to a gorge containing the small but attractive **Cane River Falls**, formerly the haunt of a runaway slave turned robber called Three Fingered Jack, who terrorised the entire area for years until his death at the hands of Quashie and his Maroons in 1781. They carried his head and hand preserved in a bucket of rum to Kingston to claim their £300 reward. After the falls, the rough, unpaved road leads eventually to Kingston at the University of the West Indies. Shortly before Yallahs the road crosses the bed of the Yallahs River on a low concrete fording. The river is only a trickle for most of the year, but the large boulders which litter the bed testify to the fact that this is not always the case, and during the wet season it is occasionally an impassable torrent. In this case a five-mile detour must be made via the bridge at *Easington*. The town of Yallahs, which takes its name from a former Spanish ranch, the Hato de Ayala, sprawls without recognisable merit along the main road. After the town on the left are the **Salt Ponds**, two shallow basins almost cut off from the sea by narrow arms of land. Due to rapid evaporation the ponds have a high salt content and resemble miniature Dead Seas. The Spaniards used

them for salt manufacture. After a permanent huddle of roadside fruit vendors, the road leaves the arid scenery at a waterfall gushing from the roadside rock at **Roselle Beach**, which boasts a small snack bar. Following a switchback stretch of road is (left) the big Goodyear factory which satisfies almost all Jamaica's tyre needs, followed by the longest bridge in the island. At the roundabout is (left) the road to **Seaforth** and, for the intrepid traveller, a rough road with spectacular views, over Hagley Gap along the Grand Ridge via Mavis Bank to Kingston. It involves driving through the Yallahs and Negro Rivers and so is impassable after heavy rains.

Immediately after the roundabout comes **Morant Bay**, which occupies a special place in Jamaica's history due to the revolt there in 1865, the cruel suppression of which influenced subsequent British colonial policies. The slaves so reluctantly freed in 1838 had, effectively, no vote, and in addition to physical hardships were unfairly dealt with by the courts. The then Governor of the island was Edward John Eyre, famous for his Australian explorations, but a poor administrator, who attributed all the miseries of the lower classes to their own laziness. A thorn in his side was **William George Gordon**, son of a Scottish planter and a slave woman. Gordon rose to be a land owner and was elected to the House of Assembly. He was also a lay preacher and founder of a Baptist sect, and was tireless in pleading the case of the common people to an unsympathetic House. One of Gordon's deacons in St

Paul Bogle (Morant Bay) by Edna Manley

Thomas, **Paul Bogle**, made many peaceful attempts to get justice for his followers including, for example, one petition ending . . . 'We therefore call upon Your Excellency for protection, seeing we are Her Majesty's loyal subjects'. After walking from St Thomas to Spanish Town in an unsuccessful attempt to gain audience with Eyre, Bogle led a mob to the court at Morant Bay and, after being fired on, attacked the Court House, burning it and killing sixteen of its defenders, including the Custos of the parish. The revolt was spontaneous and strangely idealistic; for example the leaders wasted time during the campaign collecting money to *buy* gunpowder from the local storekeeper! Reprisals were swift and harsh, with Bogle, Gordon (who appears to have had nothing to do with it) and over 440 others being executed. Attempts to bring Eyre to trial as a murderer failed, but the scandal split Britain into pro- and anti-Eyre factions, and led to his dismissal and recall. Jamaica became a

Crown Colony with subsequent social reforms not only in the island, but also in other British colonies. Paul Bogle is commemorated by a statue by Edna Manley in front of the Court House, which is reached by turning left at the park (right) up to the first (right) road which contains Courthouse, Parish Church (built in 1881) and Fort. William George Gordon and eighteen others were hanged from a boom in front of the Courthouse, while Paul Bogle and his brother were later hanged from the centre arch of the burnt out building. Excavations in 1965 behind the fort wall yielded seventy-nine skeletons, included among which must be those of Gordon and Bogle. The mass grave and monument lie under the cannon of the Fort. These three cannon are early nineteenth-century twenty-four pounders (i.e. firing a twenty-four lb. cannon ball) and the fort could (and can) accommodate nine such guns. Most of the buildings in Morant Bay were burnt during and after the 1865 revolt, and today, apart from the Courthouse area, the town is a humdrum little place, notable only for some quaint street names such as *Soul Street* or *Debtor's Lane*. Beyond the town is the white sand public beach at **Lyssons**, after which, beyond the beach development at Prospect, comes **Port Morant**, overlooking a wide harbour. The red-roofed building seen across the bay is the sugar and banana shipping terminal of Bowden. This is prime coconut and banana country, and the stately coconut palms, with the shorter, broad-leaved banana trees growing below them, stretch as far as the eye can see. Beyond Bowden on the road (right) is **Old Pera**, and the ruins of Fort Lindsay. There are plans to develop Pera, with its extensive beaches, into a resort area.

From Port Morant the road (left), via Airy Castle, leads through miles of coconut plantation to **Bath**, developed as a spa (Bath of St Thomas the Apostle) in 1699 after the discovery of thermal springs. For a while the town flourished as a fashionable resort, but public whim changed and already by 1774 accounts of Bath mention its decline. In 1779 the **Bath Botanic Garden** was established, and was the centre for the establishment and distribution of many imported plants, including Captain Bligh's breadfruit and Admiral

Rodney's mangoes. The garden was too far from Kingston to be popular, however, and after its partial destruction by the flooding of the Sulphur River, a new botanic garden was established at Castleton, and Bath Garden declined to its present size. It is now the smallest and least-visited of Jamaica's botanic gardens, but still contains many trees of interest, particularly the palms, a descendant of the original breadfruit, the giant Ceylonese *Barringtonia speciosa*, lichee and cannonball trees.

Bath follows the valley of the **Plantain Garden River** and has its centre around the junction with the Sulphur River. The Botanic Garden is on the right beside the old church, and the road directly opposite (left) leads up the Sulphur River Valley to terminate at the **Mineral Baths**. These are somewhat dilapidated, but the hot springs can be reached by a primitive track along the right hand side of the main building, then a descent down steep rough steps to the river, where the very hot springs (122°F) bubble from the rock side by side with cold mineral springs. The list of ailments these springs are claimed to cure would suggest that they will help any condition which the patient believes they will help. They are clearly heated by deep volcanic activity, and the atmosphere in the gorge is oppressively humid, resulting in the vegetation being almost primordial in its lush character. The spa shares with the Botanic Garden an impression of sadness, and everywhere are lingering echoes of greater days.

After Bath the road continues through coconut palms to Batchelor's Hall where a side road (right) goes through the cane fields to Pleasant Hill on the main road to Golden Grove. Across the main road junction beside a prominent 'Chiquita Farm' sign, a dirt road leads up to (fourth side road on the left, on a wooden knoll) **Stokes Hall Great House** ruin. In 1636 old Governor Luke Stokes brought 1 600 settlers from Nevis to settle this area but died along with the majority of them in the attempt. His sons carried on however, and Stokes Hall was probably built towards the end of the seventeenth century. Solidly built, the thick stone walls loopholed for firearms, it has a single-storied square main building with a two-storied tower at each corner. Gutted by fire forty years ago, it is now the preserve of birds, lizards and creepers, but remains for all that one of Jamaica's most compelling ruins.

Returning to the main road a right turn leads to **Golden Grove** in the midst of miles of sugar cane. At the petrol station junction the road (right) goes to Duckenfield and the distantly visible Jamaica Sugar Estate Factory. Just beyond this junction, over the little bridge is a group of attractive old buildings, relics of a former sugar estate. They include handsome arched stables with a double outside staircase, and the former book-keeper's house. Opposite the latter is the shell of a well-constructed brick church with a square clock tower. It was for this church that the estate slaves collected £20 to buy the inscribed Communion Cup which now reposes in Spanish Town Cathedral. The side road by the church leads eventually to the bathing beach at **Holland Bay** (beware of currents) and to the **Morant Point** lighthouse at the eastmost tip of the island. About 2 miles after the church on this side road is (right) a small brick slave dungeon used for the incarceration of errant slaves on the former Holland Estate. After Golden Grove comes **Hordley**, former plantation of the author 'Monk' Lewis. After inheriting it, he paid a visit in 1818 and reported 'I expected to find a perfect paradise, and I found a perfect hell . . . . . complaints of all kinds stunned me from all quarters: all the blacks accused all the whites, and all the whites accused all the blacks; and as far as I could make out, both parties were extremely in the right.' After Hordley, the road soon reaches the coast again at **Hector's River**, one of many unusual names of rivers and villages in the area, other charmers being *Cabbage Bottom, Coffee River, Christmas River, River Styx, Happy Grove* and *Sharpnose Point*.

Manchioneal is an attractive fishing village built along the shore line. Bananas and coconuts are exported from its harbour. Leaving it, the road follows the coast through the tall coconut palms and here we see widespread evidence of the sad destruction of these beautiful trees by *Lethal Yellowing Disease*, leaving only the bare dead trunks. They are being replaced by the more resistant but far less graceful dwarf palm variety. After passing through a small dark and damp fern

Coastline near Portland

gully, we emerge into the sunlight just before **Long Bay** with a breathtaking view of white capped breakers crashing on the crescent beach. This was the most wildly beautiful beach in Jamaica, with a profusion of tall palms stretching out at improbable angles over the breakers. Tragically, the disease has decimated them, and half of the beauty has gone. On the beach are 'Ports of Call' and the *Long Bay Beach Hotel.*

Slightly beyond are several beach cottages for rental. Unfortunately, there are treacherous currents at this north end of the bay, near to the hotel; the end of the beach nearer Kingston is safe. A mile after Long Bay is the picture postcard fisherman's inlet of **Priestman's River**, with the blue river meeting the sea amongst a profusion of plant and sea life. Two miles later comes **Boston Bay**, one of the finest beaches in Jamaica. Sited in an almost circular cove, with white sand, clear turquoise water and sheltered by cliffs, it offers an ideal and safe point to soak or swim away some of the sweat of the journey. There is a small bar and snack bar. Some interesting fish inhabit the rocks around the foot of the cliffs and can be observed with the aid of a mask and flippers. Boston is famous for a local food called *jerk pork*, this being rather fat pork cuts well peppered, and smoked over a slow pimento wood fire. The vendors are just off the roadside (right) immediately beyond the beach. Try a small piece before buying, as some is more pepper than pork. It costs about $1.50 per pound (seldom

weighed) and you should insist on getting at least some lean pork, as silent acceptance is the criterion of a fat lover. Next comes **Blue Hole**, visible from the road and reached by driving down a steep little road. Its blueness seems too intense to be true, and the vertigo-like effect of diving into it is exhilarating. The colour is due to sunlight penetrating far down into the depth of what is, in effect a very deep (210 ft.) hole. **San San** bay, following Blue Hole, has as its centre-piece Pellew Island, straight out of Robinson Crusoe. This very beautiful bay has good beaches, (mostly private) and many apartments and resort villages for rent (1972/3 price-range, $100 to $500 per week). The island is uninhabited and it is possible to climb down a steep track at the road bend opposite the island (beside some modern villas), to a tiny beach below, and from there swim across to the island, which has a reef behind and to the left, and is an ideal area for snorkelling. Almost opposite the island, above the main road, is the modern cottage style hotel of **Goblin Hill** which affords a panoramic view of San San.

Farther along the road is (right) the entrance to **Frenchman's Cove**, reputedly the most expensive hotel in the world, and at $1400 per person per week this could be true. For this you get an individual luxury cottage, personal butler, maid, golf cart to run around the property, all food, drink, transport, golf, tennis, water sports and entertainment. It is luxury indeed, at a price.

However, Frenchman's Cove has a central

'great house' containing ten hotel bedrooms, which in the summer season (16 April to 15 December) can be rented with three meals and use of the Frenchman's Cove facilities, for $30 per person per night. Near Frenchman's Cove are the non-millionaire cottage hotels of *Dragon Bay* and *Trident Villas*. Shortly before Port Antonio a side road (right) passes between two white gate houses and leads along the side of the bay up to **Folly**. The pillared, roofless elegance of this ruin has given rise to many legends of its origins. The most popular is that it was built by an American millionaire called Sam for his bride. Unfortunately, the builders mixed the cement with sea water, as a result of which the building began, in local parlance, to 'mash up'. Sam's bride left him, to the sound of the roof falling in. The facts, dull by comparison, are that the house was built in 1905 by a New York contractor for Alfred Mitchell of Connecticut and his long established wife (a Tiffany of New York). He lived largely at Folly until his death in 1912. The two-storied concrete building lies along the beach, and from the remnants of tiled floors and the terazzo columns, appears to have been a very elegant residence. Whether the sea water cement story is true or not, the roof did fall in (1938) because the iron reinforcing rods had corroded.

Port Antonio nestles between the mountains and a double natural harbour whose two basins are separated by the *Titchfield* peninsula. The town was originally called Titchfield after the Duke of Portland's estate in Hampshire and was founded in 1723 on the peninsula, behind the shelter of **Fort George** at the tip. Most of the fort's ten-foot thick walls still remain, together with cannon, and now enclose the buildings of Titchfield school. The half-mile long island off the peninsula is Navy Island, formerly owned by the actor Errol Flynn, who lived for years in the area. Behind the school are many appealing old houses scattered around King, Fort George and Musgrave streets. *DeMontevin Hotel* for example, on the corner of the latter two streets, is a well preserved example of period vernacular style. In the centre of the town is the **court house** a picturesque balconied building fronted by a small plaza. Opposite is *West Street* (leading out of town to the west), which has a little park a few yards up on the left, where vendors in long white aprons sell jerk pork brought in from Boston. From the court house, Harbour Street leads past the brick 1840 parish church, and a right turn up Bonnie View leads to *Bonnie View Hotel* with a superb view over the entire town and harbours. Any white ships seen in the West Harbour (left) are probably banana boats, as the port exports over half Jamaica's bananas. Unfortunately the days of 'headed' bunches and *'come mister tallyman, tally me banana, day da light, an me wan go home'* are over, and the fruit is now shipped in boxes.

The Folly of 1905

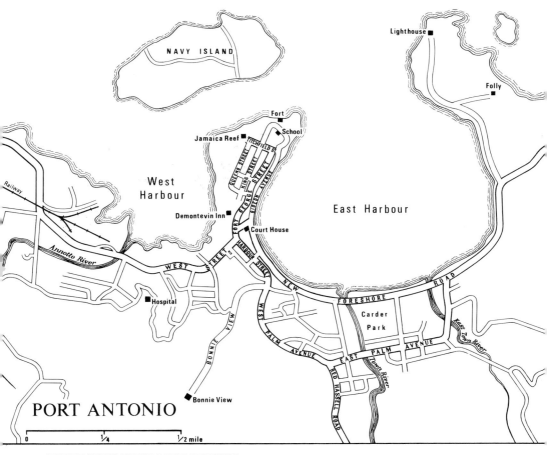

PORT ANTONIO

EXCURSIONS FROM PORT ANTONIO

The Windward Maroons

The Maroons (see page 20) occupied two main geographical areas, Portland in the east, and around the Cockpit country in the north-west. Those in Portland, the so-called **Windward Maroons**, had their bases at **Nanny Town** in the Blue Mountains and **Moore Town** in the John Crow Mountains. The Maroons occupied and controlled vast areas, striking at the white settlements on the plains almost at will, acting as a refuge for runaway slaves, and, as their numbers grew, becoming a threat to the plantation system in the east of the island. Masters of guerrilla warfare, they were more than a match for the Redcoats and Militia who were sent into the mountains to destroy them. Nanny Town was called after a warrior queen, who legend imbued with the power to catch enemy musket balls and fire them back in a shockingly unorthodox manner. It was finally taken by a Captain Stoddart and his militia, who managed to haul some field pieces on to a peak above the town, and batter it into submission. Diplomacy achieved what force of arms could not, and in 1740 a treaty with the Maroons gave them land, autonomy, and freedom from taxes, in exchange for their services against runaway and rebellious slaves, functions which they seem to have performed with surprising enthusiasm.

There are two Maroon settlements within easy reach of Port Antonio – **Moore Town** and **Cornwall Barracks**. These are reached by taking the next turning on the left after Bonnie View – Red Hassell Road, and following it for 7 miles (left fork at Fellowship)

67

Rafting on the Rio Grande, a 'must' for visitors

straight through Windsor and Seaman's Valley to Moore Town. The road beyond, to Cornwall Barracks, is rough. Superficially, Maroon settlements look like most other Jamaican villages, but apart from slight physical differences in the people, there are cultural differences, for example the music and dance of *Kumina* is exclusive to this region. The word is supposedly Arawak; the drumming, using the feet on the drum skin to alter the pitch, and the rhythm, are African, but they differ from those in any other part of Jamaica. The communities are under the control of a Colonel, who is head of the *Osofu*, or council, whose members are still summoned by blowing the Abeng horn (possibly from the Spanish *Avengo* – 'come here'). These are unique communities which have retained a tribal character and, being descended from a fusion of free Spanish speaking Negroes, Arawaks and runaway Africans from the plantations, possess an inheritance not yet completely swamped by modern cultures.

RAFTING. The rafting trip down the Rio Grande from Berridale to the sea has been described by seasoned travellers as the most impressive and delightful experience in Jamaica. The trip, which includes rapids and calm sweeps of river where a pause for a swim can be made, lasts two-and-a-half hours, and includes truly beautiful stretches of mountain and near-jungle scenery. Drive along Harbour Street to Red Hassell Road (left) then to Fellowship where the right fork leads to **Berridale** at the end of the road. Here a raft for two, under the skilled polemanship of a registered rafter, takes visitors down river to the sea at Rafters Rest, while a driver takes their car down to meet them. **Rafters Rest** has first class restaurant and bar facilities, plus a small souvenir shop. It is 5 miles west of Port Antonio.

Somerset Falls - an impressive waterfall picnic spot slightly west of Rafters Rest.

NONESUCH CAVES. These are easy caves, in that they are dry, level, and easily accessible.

Another stream – Street scene in Port Antonio

The stalagmites have been formed into a variety of fantastic shapes. For the older, or less energetic visitor, Nonesuch offers an opportunity to see on a smaller scale what the less accessible caves are like. There is a small restaurant nearby.

GAME FISHING. Port Antonio is the island centre for deep sea fishing, and one need not go too far to enjoy it, as the sea bed shelves sharply, and Blue Marlin can be caught within a mile from the shore. The record Blue Marlin catch out of Port Antonio is 600 lbs., and the town stages an annual fishing contest each year in October. Current cost of renting a deep sea boat inclusive of tackle and crew is $150 per day.

GETTING THERE. Port Antonio is the terminus of the north east **railway** line from Kingston. The route via Spanish Town, Bog Walk, Highgate, Annotto Bay and then along the coast, is both scenic and cheap ($2 return). Train times are given on page 33.

Beyond Rafters Rest, 7 miles outside Port Antonio, is *Ken Jones Airfield*, which is served by Jamaica Air Service twice daily ($16 return). It is also possible to charter a small three or five seater aircraft ($60 or $90) for group excursions.

Leaving Port Antonio by way of West Street and Rafters Rest **the road** follows the north coast westwards to Buff Bay where a side road (left) leads through the heart of the Blue Mountains over Newcastle to Kingston. The road is partially unpaved, and may be impassable after heavy rains, but it possesses turbulent beauty, and exposes a face of Jamaica entirely different from the rest of the route. There are no petrol stations between Buff Bay and Kingston on this road. The coast road crosses the iron bridge at Buff Bay and continues to Annotto Bay, where the Junction Road (left) leads to Kingston. A couple of miles before Annotto Bay, on the left, is the fine old Great House of Iter Boreale, whose seventeenth-century cellars are now a cool and pleasant bar. Meals are also available and the house contains a small museum of Arawak relics.

NORTH COAST

Castleton Gardens, Highgate, Annotto Bay, Port Maria, Linstead

Leaving Kingston through the northern suburb of Stony Hill, the route includes Castleton Botanic Gardens and follows the winding course of the Wag Water River to the quiet, rather straggling town of Annotto Bay on the North Coast. A detour through the interior uplands includes Highgate, a cool pleasant township, and reaches the coast at Port Maria, near which the large Brimmer Hall plantation can be visited. The road follows the coastline closely, and after the port of Oracabessa enters a stretch which becomes more tourist-oriented as we approach Ocho Rios. The return to Kingston can be made via Ocho Rios, Fern Gully, Mount Diablo, Moneague and Linstead, or, for those who prefer quiet byways to busy highways, by turning off at Rio Nuevo, halfway between Oracabessa and Ocho Rios and proceeding down the rough-but-drivable B3 via Guy's Hill and Devil's Racecourse to Linstead, made famous in the folk song 'Linstead Market'. Three miles beyond is Bog Walk, at the end of the gorge of the Rio Cobre. From here, there are two routes back to Kingston. The major one is through the gorge, across the old Spanish Flat Bridge, and through Spanish Town, while the minor and quieter road climbs into the hills via Sligoville and Rock Hall, descending on the city, with a panoramic view over the entire plain, via Red Hills. Unless you want to visit Spanish Town, this is the road to take.

ROUTE

From Halfway Tree we follow Hagley Park Road down to the first traffic lights, then turn right along Eastwood Park Road until a slight rise takes us up to the main Constant Spring Road, where we turn left. Follow the main road to a Y junction at a petrol station (Mary Brown's Corner) where we bear right up through Manor Park, eventually veering left up the Old Stony Hill Road. This winds up by Red Gal Ring past select Stony Hill, and through the township of **Golden Spring** where the road to the right via Mount Airy makes a rough but scenic detour through the hills, following the Wag Water River for part of the way, and rejoining the main road 5 miles farther on at Coakley, 4 miles before **Castleton Botanic Gardens**. Enjoying a beautiful setting in the broad valley of the Wag Water, these gardens were founded in 1862, and cover fifteen acres which are bisected by the main road. The portion to our left contains the former palmetum, arboretum, formal gardens and lily pond, and is packed with exotic imported trees, shrubs and flowers (details and locations are given in Alan Eyre's little book, see page 3). Castleton has over 100 inches of rain per year, with May, October, November and December the wettest months, so take some protection during these periods. The right-hand side of the gardens extend past a

little cafeteria down to the banks of the Wag Water, where it is possible to take a cooling dip. The river is normally quiet and placid, but the huge boulders strewn about its bed reveal that this is not always so, and, in fact, large tracts of the gardens have been washed away during heavy rains.

After Castleton, the road follows the tortuous course of the Wag Water, whose name is said to derive from the Arawak name of *Guayguata*. A laudable English attempt to bend this into a Spanish name produced *Rio de la Agua Alta*, and hence *Agualta Vale*, farther along. After the gardens, the road is serpentine, so stay well over on your own side and sound your horn loud and clear before the bends. After a few miles of winding narrow gorge, the river course opens out into a broad flat valley planted with bananas and coconut palms. Eight miles after Castleton, at **Chovey**, the road to the left over the narrow silvery bridge climbs up into the hills to **Highgate**. The road rises steadily through vast coconut and banana plantations interspersed with pasture land, and passes through the hamlets of Lewis Store, Clonmel and Clermont, to the township of Highgate, built between 800 and 1 000 ft. up and down the sides of the hills. On entering the outskirts, (for, like most Jamaican towns, it is a sprawling little empire), we meet a petrol station on the left, opposite a Quaker (Society of Friends) church on the right. The small road to the left of the church leads up to two places of artistic interest. In the early 1950's an American millionairess had the excellent idea of founding an artists' colony in Highgate. Unfortunately, she died before it got going, but two of the original colonists are to be found up this little road. They are at the *Friends Craft Centre*, the focal point of a cottage industry complex which produces high quality furniture from local hardwoods and raffia. Even if you have no intention of taking a chair or table home with you, it is worth having a look at these well-designed products. Next door a sign points to the *2 Todds*, this being the pottery studio and showroom of Edwin and Maribel Todd, who produce artistic and reasonably priced pottery, some of it finished in new types of glaze produced from a variety of local mineral and vegetable materials. The Todds are happy to see visitors, especially musically inclined ones, as they themselves are accomplished musicians (cello and violin). The view from the lawn, of the distant Blue Mountains, is one of the finest vistas in Jamaica. At the end of the main street is Highgate Market, a ramshackle open-sided erection in stark contrast to the neat modern shopping centre a few yards below it. The road to the left of the market leads via Dean Pen and Windsor Castle, to Guy's Hill on the interior road back to Linstead. Passing to the right of the market we descend past the *Cranleigh School for Young Ladies and Gentlemen* and eventually through still more coconut and banana (the parish of St Mary is the island's leading producer of both) for 8 miles to Port Maria. A mile before the town a well signposted road on the left leads to **Brimmer Hall** where Plantation Tours take place daily at 11 a.m., 1.30 p.m., and 3.30 p.m. except Saturdays. This is a well organized operation and in addition to the motorised tour there is a restaurant, bar, swimming pool, boutique gift shops etc.

Port Maria is the main town of the parish and has the expected court house and parish church. The town is in two parts joined by a bridge. The first part is a busy shopping area centred on a road junction. We turn left at the petrol station and across the bridge to the quieter and older part of town. The road follows the coastline past the sea-sprayed Presbyterian church, which enjoys one of the most romantic settings of any church in the island, and was built by a local planter for the minister he was bringing out to preach to his slaves. This stretch of road runs along high above the sea, and affords some beautiful views of the rugged coastline in this area. Seven miles farther along the coast is the port of **Oracabessa** (*Golden Head* in Spanish, *oro* gold and *cabeza* head). The road divides on entering the town, re-uniting again on the far side. Take the right hand coast road, which passes by the gates, recognisable by the large bronze pineapples on top of **Golden Eye**, home of the late Ian Fleming, and the place where most of the *James Bond* novels were written. Noel Coward was also a regular winter resident of the area.

Beyond the town is **Boscobel** air strip, and a mile farther on Jamaica's Playboy Club. After 2½ miles the road crosses the Rio Nuevo, scene of the Spanish defeat by the English which effectively ended their hopes of regaining the island. The side road on the left immediately beyond the river is the B13 route to Linstead via Gayle. The main A1 carries on to Ocho Rios where a left turn at the roundabout would take us up through Fern Gully and over Mount Diablo through Ewarton to Linstead. The B13 is a quieter and more picturesque route, which winds up into the seldom visited St Mary uplands, following the Rio Nuevo Valley up to Gayle then on to the village of Guy's Hill where it meets the side road (left) to Highgate. Next come the exuberant convolutions of the stretch of road known as *Devil's Racecourse*. After 11 miles of undulating country, bearing the smallholders' usual variety of crops in small patches, we descend to the broad valley of St Thomas in Ye Vale, and enter the busy local centre of **Linstead**. The market is half way along the main street on the east (left) side, beneath a little square clock tower. The song *Linstead Market* tells the simple story of a market woman who carried her produce there but had to take it home again without making a sale.

'Carry me ackee go a Linstead Market,
not a quattie wut sell (repeat)
Oh lawd not a mite not a bite,
Wat a Satiday night!'

Linstead was built for more leisurely days,
and under the pressures of modern traffic,
south bound vehicles must detour through
some side streets. A stretch of cane fields
separates Linstead from Bog Walk which
houses Jamaica's only milk condensery and
also United Estates Sugar Factory. Beyond
the town the road crosses an iron bridge over
the Rio Pedro, at the end of which a road on
the left leads to Sligoville. The main A1 road
follows the Rio Cobre gorge crossing the river
by the Flat Bridge, a low-down Spanish relic.
It stands only a few feet above the normal
water level, and after heavy rains it is
frequently impassable. On a rock face beside

the bridge is marked the water level reached
in 1933, 25 ft. above the bridge.

The Sligoville road is free from such
exciting possibilities, climbing steadily out of
the valley into the hills (look back for a
splendid view of St Thomas in Ye Vale), then
roller-coasting to Kingston. At the village of
Sligoville bear left at the junction (right goes
to Spanish Town) and continue through the
smallholding-dotted countryside to Rock
Hall, where we go to the right of the
prominent petrol station for Kingston via Red
Hills, a village which, although the capital is
almost on top of it, has managed to retain its
rural character. During the steep descent to
Kingston some truly spectacular panoramas
of the Blue Mountains and the entire
Liguanea Plain present themselves. We enter
the metropolis via Red Hills Road, Constant
Spring Road, and thence to Half Way Tree.

Area 5   NORTH COAST

Moneague, Ocho Rios, St. Ann's Bay, Brown's Town, Good Hope, Falmouth

These routes encompass two contrasting aspects of Jamaica: the coast, with palm fringed
beaches and fishing villages interspersed with tourist resorts and modern hotels; and the
interior, tourist-free small towns and hamlets whose people earn a simple but seemingly
adequate living from the soil. Both aspects are covered by the twin routes given — one along
the coast (the A1), the other inland (B11) and almost parallel to the coast. They are connected
by many cross roads, so stretches of each can be covered if time is short. The coast road
includes tourist areas, beaches, and the Columbus country, while the interior route reveals
more typical Jamaican life, and a variety of its scenery.

INLAND ROUTE. The A1 from Spanish
Town passes through **Moneague**, where a side
road (left) leads through Friendship and
Pedro to Jamaica's most macabre ruin,
Edinburgh Castle. This is the remains of a hill
tower from which, in the 1760's Lewis
Hutchinson, a sadistic red-haired Scottish
ex-medical student, murdered over forty
travellers by shooting at them from the slit
windows of his tower. The robbed,
decapitated bodies were allegedly thrown
down a nearby sink hole. Captured whilst
trying to board a ship off shore, the un-
repentant Hutchinson, before he was hanged,
brazenly left £100 for the erection of a
monument to himself bearing the inscription
'Their sentence, pride and malice I defy;
Despise their power, and like a Roman die'. It

was never erected. From Moneague the road
goes (left) to Claremont, where we bear right
at the little clock tower, then take the first
left, a couple of miles beyond the town. This
is the B11 to Bamboo and Brown's Town (the
A1 continues ahead to St Ann's Bay). The
first largish community is Bamboo, sitting
high among the hills at 2 000 ft., a prominent
radio mast towering over it. **Brown's Town**,
built on the hillsides at the convergence of
several valleys, has at its centre a large
market, where our road meets the north/
south road from Discovery Bay to May Pen.
On entering, we drive straight across the first
road junction, then right at the market,
with its small, quaint clock tower, and downhill to the main street. Facing the market is St
Mark's Church, an arresting nineteenth-

century Gothic structure. In the main street the post office and police station are twins, each stone-arched and balconied, with tile roofs, giving an almost Spanish effect to the street. Above them, reached by a steep side street, is the Georgian court house, well-built in cut stone, with pillared portico and Adams frieze. Brown's Town is unusual among Jamaican towns in being built on many levels, which gives it something of a Mediterranean character, and makes walking around it a stimulating, if exhausting experience. After leaving it, we enter rolling, fertile country, which supports hundreds of small settlers, whose little brightly coloured houses cling to the steep green slopes in some truly improbable positions, creating scenes reminiscent of a child's painting.

Stewart Town comes next, with three churches, one of which, St Thomas, can be seen in the grassy valley far below the road. It is unusual, if not unique, in Jamaica in having 'crow step' gables. The adjacent ruins are an old saw mill. Beyond the church, a road (right) leads to Discovery Bay. Two miles along this road, about 200 yards beyond a 'Dornoch' sign, a rough steep track (left) leads down to **Riverhead** – the source of the Rio Bueno. Here, under a stark cliff face, the river rises out of the earth into a deep pool, and flows silently off to the sea. After Stewart Town the road descends to Jackson Town on the fringe of the Trelawny canefields, thence to Clark's Town whose sole claim to attention is St Michael's, an attractive Anglican church built at the time of Emancipation. Just in front of the church, we meet the north/south B.10 with the road (right) going through Clark's Town heart via *Long Pond Sugar Factory and Distillery* (they make Gold Label rum) to Duncans on the coast. The unpaved road to the left (B.10) leads to Troy and Oxford. Two miles along it, at Kinloss, a side road (right) goes via Sherwood Content and Bunkers Hill to Wakefield. At Sherwood Content a rough(er) road (left) leads to **Windsor Cave** in the Cockpit Country. This cave is 1½ miles deep, but only the first two lofty chambers are easily negotiable, and they are rich in bat manure. For the young, fit and truly adventurous, there is a track (left) branching from the path up to the cave, which leads

St. Marks, Brown's Town

through the Cockpits to Troy 10 miles away on the B.10. The going is extremely rough, and take a compass, as there will be no one to help you if you get lost. Approximately 5 miles after Sherwood Content, a side road (right) leads to **Good Hope Estate**, one of the most beautiful and interesting on the island. First we encounter the ruins of the sugar factory, grouped around an elegant stone bridge with a superstructure of square columns bearing wrought iron brackets. On the near bank of the river (Martha Brae) is the almost perfectly preserved water wheel of the mill house, and on the far bank the other factory buildings, one of which is now used as a copra (coconut meat) factory. Following the road, we arrive at a group of handsome Georgian buildings. On the right is the estate office with, 100 yards or so behind it, the ruins of the Slave Hospital, a vast, impressive edifice on two floors, and as can be seen from a print in the Great House, a very fine

73

building in its day. The estate is scattered with truly beautiful old buildings, so it is fitting that **Good Hope Great House** should be one of the handsomest on the island. Built around 1755, it has a double-staired portico with two flanking wings and a steeply pitched shingled roof. The interior is high-ceilinged and spacious, giving an idea of how gracious living in the great days of the plantocracy could be. Behind the house is the intriguing Counting House, a square two-storied stone building. The lower storey is a low, vaulted chamber, whose shape and thick iron studded door, with ventilation holes, suggest that it was a slave dungeon. The estate is opened as an hotel during the winter season, with accommodation in a block behind the Great House. Horseback tours over the 6 000 acres are a specialty.

Continuing north we come to the village of **Martha Brae**, where the side road (right) leads to the **Rafter's Village** a mile up river. Sited at the neck of an oxbow in the Martha Brae River, the village is a pleasingly well planned unit, containing the starting point for the one-and-a-half hour rafting trip down to the terminus, where rafters are collected and driven back to the village, which has restaurant, bar, boutiques, souvenir shops etc. The main road continues past Martha Brae to Falmouth, a mile away. The road from Clark's Town through Bunker's Hill (i.e. after the right turn to Good Hope) passes Wakefield, then through the canefields of the Queen of Spain's Valley and the **Hampden Sugar Factory**, on the boundary between Trelawny and St James parishes. The factory has tours for visitors on Tuesdays and Thursdays. Leaving the valley at Adelphi where we take the road (right) which leads to the coast near to Falmouth, passing impressive sugar factory ruins at Kent and (particularly) **Orange Valley**. The main road (i.e. straight ahead) at Adelphi follows the cool, shady valley of the Montego River through Sign, where the Great House has been turned into a luxury hotel.

THE COAST ROUTE Approaching Moneague our road goes right of the Esso station (i.e. straight ahead) for 12 miles to Ocho Rios. The countryside is undulating pasture with glimpses of great houses perched on distant hills, and after 8 miles we enter **Fern Gully** and follow it down to the outskirts of Ocho Rios. The gully, formerly a river bed, is deep, with a profusion of ferns, fern trees and trees shutting out the sunlight. Picturesque as it is, the road can be very slippery, particularly after rain, due to some substance washed out of the soil or vegetation, and you are advised to take it slowly in low gear. The fern population is less than a few years ago, and it appears that vandals and car exhaust fumes are taking their toll. **Ocho Rios** (Eight Rivers) is a misnomer as there never was this number in the area. The true Spanish name was *Las Chorroras* — 'the waterfalls'. The English, mis-comprehending, and applying elementary Spanish, got Ocho Rios. Shortly before the town, a signposted road (left) leads to **Shaw Park Gardens**, landscaped, with a rushing stream, tall old trees and flowering shrubs, and with a vista of bay and town. Ocho Rios is not really a town, but a village overtaken by tourist development, and its hotels, houses and shops are strung out along the coast road like beads on a string. Our road meets a roundabout near the water's edge, with most of the town to the right of it. Ocho Rios is growing fast, and now has four multi-storey blocks of tourist apartments, and, farther along the road, right of the roundabout, the shopping centre of Pineapple Place, with everything from 'Native Wood Carvings' to a 'Scottish Shop'. Across the road are less sophisticated local shops. Beyond Pineapple Place is the hotel area, containing the *Jamaica Inn Tower Isle Hotel*, and the *Playboy Club*.

Our route goes left at the roundabout, passing the giant sugar bulk loading terminal and bauxite loading berth, and on to **Dunn's River Falls**, where the river falls 600 ft. over polished stones, and passes under the main road to the beach. The falls are spectacular, and are easily climbed, even against the cascading cold water. This water cools the sea near the beach, which is good but busy. After Dunn's River comes (right) *Jamaica Hilton Hotel*, well appointed on its private beach followed just before the side road (left) to Steer Town by **Drax Hall**, an old sugar estate now given over to cattle and coconuts. It is the scene of Saturday afternoon polo matches. The property includes an inlet called Don Christopher's Cove, not after Columbus, but the leader of the Spanish Guerrillas, Don Cristobel Isassi (see page 20). We are now entering Columbus Country. **St Ann's Bay** is the starting point of Jamaica's history, being **Columbus's** first anchorage, the scene of his later enforced stay, and site of the first Spanish settlement in Jamaica. The capital of the parish, it is unexceptionally pleasant, one of the few buildings of note being the 1866 court house (left) above the main road beside the parish church. Beyond the town (left) at a junction, is a statue of Columbus, cast in his native Genoa. Behind is the catholic church, built of stones from various local sources, including the ruin of the original Spanish church of Peter Martyr, a soldier priest, which stood slightly to the west of the present church. The first Spanish settlement of *Sevilla Nueva* was planned on a grand scale.

Castle ruins have recently been uncovered among the coconut trees down a little dirt road (with a gate) which crosses the main road (right) just beyond the Columbus statue, (along the road take the first track to the right.) To the left of the castle are the ruins of a Spanish sugar mill which was certainly the first in Jamaica. The little road continues to the left of the main road, leading up to the ruins of an old sugar factory, overlooked by the Overseer (*busha*)'s house of Seville Estate. The track to the right of the *busha*'s house leads eventually to **Seville Great House**, set amongst the trees. Built in 1745, the house has recently been restored as a museum, and it is hoped that the Spanish carved stone friezes, door jambs, pilasters and other artifacts recovered from Sevilla Nueva and at present in the Institute of Jamaica will soon be on display there. Four miles beyond Columbus, leave the new highway to follow (right) the older coast road where, after a little bridge over the Llandovery River, a dirt road (right) leading down past a miniature Dunn's River Falls to the ruin of *Llandovery Sugar Factory*, founded in 1674, which has a colourful coat of arms above the door.

Runaway Bay, so called because the last Spaniards left Jamaica from here, after their final defeat by the English, is a booming tourist area. On entering (right) is a settlement of small conical habitations, like a Hottentot housing scheme. This is *Club Caribbean*, tourist accommodation with individual cottages arranged around a central clubhouse, containing restaurant and bar. Next (right) is *Runaway Bay Hotel*, most expensive in the area, with an eighteen-hole golf course (open to non-residents), followed by a string of smaller hotels and guest houses, of which **Eaton Hall** (right) is notable for being built on the foundations of an old English fort, complete with underground passage to the cliffs. Beaches and hotels are Runaway Bay's claim to fame; as a town it is non-existent. Well signposted beyond are **Runaway Caves**, the most accessible of Jamaica's large limestone caves. Guided tours, for $2, include some of the 1½ miles of caverns, and a sail across the grotto, 120 ft. lower.

Cunning lighting brings out the grotesque beauty of the stalactites (point down) and stalagmites (point up). Outside the caves is a 160 ft. deep lagoon. **Discovery Bay**, 5 miles farther on, is slowly developing under the stimulus of nearby Kaiser Bauxite, but its gains on the bauxite roundabouts are offset by losses on the tourism swings, which are damped by the presence of a great dusty bauxite shipping terminal bang in the middle of the bay. **Puerto Seco** beach (right on entering) is open to visitors and has restaurant facilities. Opposite is *Columbus Plaza*, with bank, bar, supermarket, etc. The town's name comes from its claim that this was where Columbus first landed in 1494, calling it, on account of the lack of water, 'Dry Harbour' (*Puerto Seco*). Beyond the bauxite terminal, Port Rhodes, with its huge green storage dome, is (right) on the cliffs **Columbus Park**.

Here are displayed cannon, sugar mill fragments including a water wheel and the old cast iron pans used for boiling juice down to sugar, and, among other items, a stone crest of Clan Campbell of Argyll, dated 1774, and taken from Knapdale in St Ann. The road crosses the Rio Bueno river by Bengal Bridge — a stylish stone structure of 1798 which serves as a boundary marker between St Ann and Trelawny parishes. **Rio Bueno**, in a bay at the mouth of the river of the same name, also has a claim to be Columbus's landing site. It is

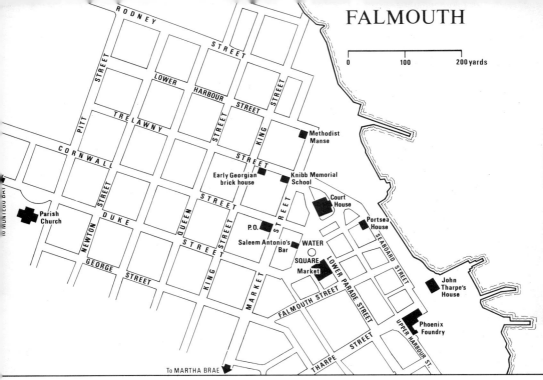

0   100   200 yards

RODNEY STREET

LOWER HARBOUR STREET

PITT STREET

TRELAWNY STREET

KING STREET

CORNWALL STREET

Methodist Manse

Early Georgian brick house

Knibb Memorial School

Court House

Parish Church

DUKE STREET

NEWTON STREET

QUEEN STREET

P.O.

Saleem Antonio's Bar

WATER SQUARE

Market

Portsea House

SEABOARD STREET

John Tharpe's House

GEORGE STREET

KING STREET

MARKET STREET

LOWER PARADE STREET

Phoenix Foundry

TO MONTEGO BAY

To MARTHA BRAE

UPPER HARBOUR ST.

THARPE STREET

an unspoilt fishing village, the main street of which has some old stone houses and is quite an art centre, containing the well-known Jamaican artist Gloria Escoffery's *Wayfarers' Gallery* (left) after the *Gallery Jo James* (right), with its little jetty behind, where it is possible to get light though rather expensive meals. St Mark's church at the water's edge, fronted by its little walled churchyard, is photogenic and has inside a J.B. Kidd print of how Rio Bueno looked in the 1830s. Beside the house next to the police station is a turtle crawl, this being a stone cavity fed with sea water by a narrow channel, in which captured turtles could be kept alive until wanted. At the far end of town (right) is Fort Dundas, built in 1778 to command both sea and bay.

The broad highway from Rio Bueno passes Braco airstrip, and reaches (6 miles) Duncans, where, at the clock tower, the road (left) leads, via Long Pond Sugar Factory and Distillery (Gold Label rum is made there) to Clark's Town on the interior road. We turn right at the clock tower, and the next right leads down to *Silver Sands Beach Club* whose beach, restaurant and bar (sit under a palm

tree on the beach) make a good pausing point for meal, drink or swim. A few miles farther along the main road is *Coral Springs* tourist resort (right). Set back from the road (left) is *Cliff Leeming's Steak House* owned by an eccentric Englishman who serves good food, including an Aphrodisiac Sea Food Soup. Behind is the ruin of a small sugar mill (Jamaica had 720 once). At *Rock*, sited on the Phosphorescent Lagoon, is *Fisherman's Inn*, a good quality restaurant specialising in sea food. After a stretch of swamp which is being reclaimed for the site of 'New Falmouth resort city', we cross the Martha Brae River and enter **Falmouth**, one of the most attractive towns in Jamaica.

Falmouth was built as a sugar port during a period of wealth and good taste, and this is reflected in the orderly plan of the town, with its broad streets and well built stone and wood houses. The Georgian heritage here is better preserved than anywhere else in the island and is more easily seen, on account of the smallness of the town. We enter via Upper Harbour Street, and the quaint beehive edifice (right) on the corner, is the 1801

Court House, Falmouth

Phoenix Foundry, one of the earliest in Jamaica. Turn left, then sharp right along Lower Parade Street to the central Water Square with its small ornamental fountain. It is advisable to park here and view the town on foot. Falmouth's bustling market occupies a side of the square, spilling out of its confines into the streets around. The greatest concentration of Georgian buildings is on Market Street; they include the Post Office, whose well balanced upper window pattern sits on a bold support of semi-circular arches. Down at the bottom of the street (left) is the Methodist Manse built by the Barretts in 1799. Elizabeth Barrett Browning, whose elopement with the poet Robert Browning is the subject of the famous play 'The Barretts of Wimpole Street', was a descendant of this family. The stone and wood house has elegant wrought iron balconies and contains excellent Adam style doorways and friezes. It is undergoing nick-of-time restoration. To the right, adjacent to Water Square, is the 1815 court house, still one of the finest Georgian buildings in Jamaica, despite poor restoration after

a fire in 1926. The portico is reached by a double exterior staircase, with the pediment supported by four doric columns. It now houses the offices of the town council. Although poverty and neglect have taken their toll, Falmouth is still a fascinating town, full of eighteenth and nineteenth-century buildings, and to stroll through its broad streets is to step into Jamaica's past. As we leave the town, Market Street goes (left) up to Martha Brae a mile away (see p. 74).

Twelve miles beyond Falmouth (left) is **Rose Hall Great House**, renowned as the abode of Annie Palmer, the Irish White Witch, who murdered three of her four husbands, had slave lovers, tortured and killed slaves, kept the head of a beautiful slave girl preserved in spirits, and was finally found strangled in bed, allegedly by slave and/or lover. It's a good story. A *great* story. But it's not a true story. There *was* an Annie Palmer at Rose Hall, but she wasn't Irish, she had only one husband, and died a respected citizen, peacefully in 1846 and is buried in Montego Bay churchyard. There *was* a mistress of Rose Hall who had Irish connections and four husbands, but she kept the last one for 23 years, and he buried her at the ripe old age (for having slave lovers) of 72, also in Montego Bay churchyard, with a eulogistic monument to her virtue inside the church. She was Rosa Palmer. Who, then, was the prototype for the 'White Witch'? Legends appear to be like gods in that, if they don't exist they must be invented, and the Rose Hall legend seems to be the result of several fertile imaginations applied to the 1830 observation of a Scottish missionary that, at the neighbouring estate of Palmyra (same owner) he saw 'the iron collars and spikes used by a lady owner there for the necks of her slaves, and also the bed on which she was found dead one morning, having been strangled'. Rose Hall is one of the largest, best designed and constructed houses in Jamaica.

Built in 1760 during the great days of sugar, it occupies a commanding position on the hillside above the canefields. After lying as a derelict, roofless ruin for years, the house has recently been completely and authentically restored by its American owner at a cost of $1½ million. It may be visited on payment of a $2 non-returnable deposit. The side road leading from the main road up to Rose Hall continues past the house, by the walled burial ground of the Moulton Barrett family, 200 yards below the road, and up to the family Great House, **Cinnamon Hill**, which with skilful restoration has retained its character and charm. It has a unique stone hurricane shelter, projecting from the house like the bow of a ship into the usual storm direction, providing a secure hurricane refuge for the family — rather like an eighteenth-century air raid shelter. Beyond Rose Hall is the highly developed tourist area centring on **Montego Bay**.

Area 6   THE WEST END

Montego Bay, Tryall, Kenilworth, Lucea, Negril, Savanna-la-Mar

MONTEGO BAY is the tourist capital of Jamaica. Consequently, it is the least Jamaican part of the island — the 'Independent Republic of Montego Bay' — where it is easier to pay in U.S. dollars than in Jamaican. Under the impact of so many wealthy (by Jamaican standards) visitors, some of the local population have adopted an unfortunately mercenary and sometimes truculent attitude, and the generally high level of prices in and around Montego Bay makes it unpopular with the majority of Jamaicans.

Architecturally, Montego Bay has much less to offer than neighbouring Falmouth. Tourists come for sun, sand and comfortable hotels, and there is little else. Beyond Montego Bay to the west the route passes Tryall Club and golf course, then by Jamaica's most impressive sugar ruins at Kenilworth, through the little town of Lucea with its circular harbour, guarded by a fort which never fired a shot in anger. From here it follows the longest and finest stretch of beach in Jamaica at Negril, and finally, through the vast cane plantations of Frome, Jamaica's biggest sugar factory, reaches Savanna-la-Mar, a sugar shipping port on the south coast.

The name Montego is said to come from the Spanish *manteca* meaning lard, as during the Spanish occupation the bay was used for shipping fat from wild and domesticated pigs and cattle. **Montego Bay** is entered from Falmouth and the east, the A1 passing through the hotel suburbs of the town, including *Rose Hall* and *Holiday Inn*, the largest hotel in the island. Passing to the

seaward of *Sangster Airport* we traverse the hotel area; half way along this road is **Doctor's Cave Beach** the spot which triggered off Montego Bay's boom as a tourist centre. Originally a cliff overhang (since collapsed) formed a virtual cave over the beach which was owned and used by a local physician, Dr. McCatty, after whom it was respectfully named. In the 1920's a claim by an English

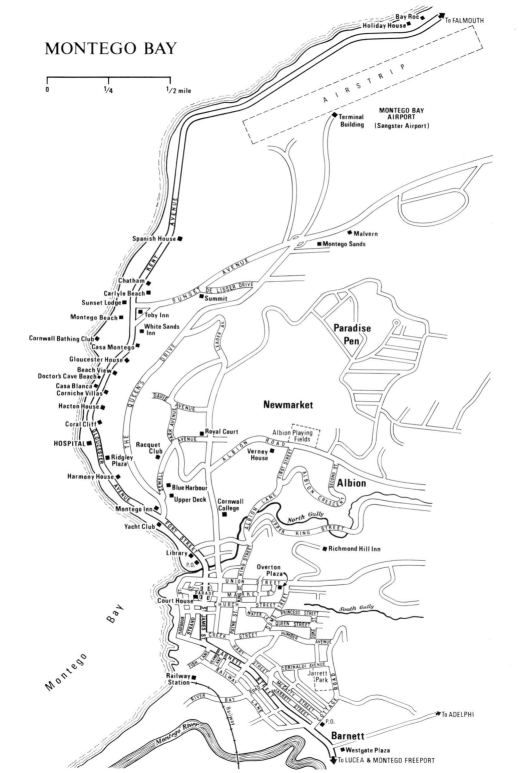

MONTEGO BAY

0 1/4 1/2 mile

To FALMOUTH
Bay Roc
Holiday House

AIRSTRIP

Terminal Building

MONTEGO BAY AIRPORT
(Sangster Airport)

Spanish House

KENT AVENUE

Malvern
Montego Sands

SUNSET AVENUE
Chatham
DE LISSER DRIVE
Carlyle Beach
Summit
Sunset Lodge
Montego Beach
Toby Inn
White Sands Inn
Cornwall Bathing Club
Casa Montego
Gloucester House
Beach View
Doctor's Cave Beach
Casa Blanca
Corniche Villas
Hacton House
Coral Cliff

THE QUEENS DRIVE

LEADER AV.

Paradise Pen

Newmarket

DAVIS AVENUE
PARK AVENUE
AVENUE
Royal Court
Racquet Club

HOSPITAL
GLOUCESTER AVENUE
Ridgley Plaza
Harmony House

SEWELL

ALBION ROAD
Albion Playing Fields
Verney House
FIRST STREET
SECOND ST.
ALBION CRESCENT
Albion

FORT STREET
Montego Inn
Blue Harbour
Upper Deck
Cornwall College
ALBION LANE
UPPER KING STREET
North Gully

Yacht Club

Library
P.O.

Richmond Hill Inn

KING STREET
Overton Plaza
UNION STREET
PARADE
MARKET ST.
CHURCH STREET
STRAND ST.
HARBOUR ST.
JAMES ST.
Court House
PAYNE ST.
WATER LANE
Princess Street
Queen Street
HUMBER AVENUE
CREEK STREET
TILT
South Gully

Montego Bay

BARNETT STREET
FISH LANE
RAILWAY LANE
Railway Station
RAILWAY
BAY
CORINALDI AVENUE
McFEE STREET
JARRETT STREET
Jarrett Park
COTTAGE ROAD
P.O.
To ADELPHI

RIVER BAY RAILWAY

Montego River

Barnett

Westgate Plaza
To LUCEA & MONTEGO FREEPORT

Montego Bay, the old Waterfront,

osteopath that the water had curative properties stimulated a rush to the beach, and Montego Bay, that has accelerated until the present day.

After the hotel area comes the town centre, with Harbour Street following the shore in front of a new hotel and tourist area development along the sea front on the former site of some interesting old warehouses and wharves. Among the surviving old buildings is the **Cage** in the north-west corner of the town square, dating from 1807 and formerly used for the detention of runaway or errant slaves. The **Slave Ring** at the corner of East and Union Streets occupies the site of a former slave market.

Montego Bay is centrally placed for some interesting excursions, including **An evening on the Great River** each Tuesday and Thursday when a Tourist Board minibus collects participants from their hotels, and takes them 10 miles west to the Great River, whence a barbecue and folklore show is reached by canoe. The setting is beautiful. Plantation tours include **Good Hope** (due north of Falmouth) and **Sign Great House** (5 miles from Montego Bay on the road to Adelphi). Between Saltmarsh and Falmouth is a **crocodile and alligator** farm run by a young American who has taught the animals a variety of simple tricks; his *piece de resistance* is a wrestling match with large crocodiles. (Tours at 10 a.m. and 4 p.m., except Mondays). Bird lovers should visit Lisa Salmon's **Rocklands Feeding Station** where, at 4 p.m. daily, hundreds of Jamaican birds of all types gather for feeding. The station is reached by driving west to Reading, then left towards Anchovy. After 2.2 miles, look for a signpost on the left indicating the road to Rock Pleasant. Half a mile along this road, Rocklands is the first gate on the right. Sea trips on the fifty passenger catamaran *Manta Ray* leaves Casa Blanca Hotel daily at 2.30 p.m. The cruise lasts three hours, including stops for swimming and snorkelling, and there is a bar on board. **Rose Hall Great House** is 7 miles east of Montego Bay on the Falmouth Road.

THE COAST ROAD. Following a series of one way streets westwards through Montego Bay (a new road system is planned) the route passes Westgate Shopping Centre (left) on the outskirts of town and after skirting the Barnett Estate cane fields, proceeds 12 miles (past Reading junction) to the roadside water wheel at **Tryall**, a one time sugar factory which was rebuilt in 1834 after being destroyed in the slave uprising of 1832. Tryall is now an upper-price-bracket hotel and golf club. Four miles beyond is one of the most impressive ruins in Jamaica. This is the sugar factory at **Kenilworth**, set back a mile to the left of the main road, up a track through cane and coconut. The first of the massive stone and brick buildings is the two storey mill house, with the housing for the water wheel which once drove the great rollers. Behind is the sugar-boiling house and distillery, a long building with two wings. Built in contrasting dark and light stone, with Palladian doors and windows, Kenilworth gets few visitors but it is well worth the trip in spite of an ugly concrete youth camp adjacent to the ruins, and in fact occupying some of them. Twenty-five miles beyond Montego Bay is **Lucea**, a quiet, unspoilt little town built on a beautiful horseshoe-shaped harbour. Once a busy sugar port, it now ships bananas and molasses and has the distinction of being the capital of Jamaica's smallest parish (Hanover). The road follows the harbour wall to the right of the court house, a stone and wood structure surmounted by an attractive columned clock tower. Beyond this, up a slight hill is (right) the entrance to **Fort Charlotte** whose cannon command the entrance to a harbour which no enemy ever tried to enter. The nearby Rusea School was established by the legacy of a grateful French refugee. Four miles beyond Lucea, above Lance's Bay, is *Pimento Cove*, a magnificently sited Great House converted by its owner Mrs. Junor, into a beautiful little hotel. After Lucea the road follows the coast past small coves and fishing beaches, first hugging the shore, then cutting inland through the sugar cane to emerge back on the coast at Green Island, a straggling township where the road (left) goes to Frome and Savanna-la-Mar. Five miles beyond begins **Negril Beach**, more than 7 miles of sparsely populated white sand, lapped by clear, still water. At present it has only one hotel, the *Sundowner*, half-way along on the beach side of the road. Water sport facilities are available, including hire of diving and snorkelling equipment. Trips out to the impressive reef can be made either in a motor boat, or, more leisurely and romantically, a local fisherman will paddle you out in his dug-out canoe.

Beyond the Sundowner are a series of beach-cottage colonies. For families or groups they are much cheaper than the hotel, and have the added advantage of privacy. Crystal Waters, Carabella and T-Water cottages are of this type. Negril has, in recent years, become a winter paradise for hippies. They live on the beach and in huts and tents along the coast between Negril village and the lighthouse at Negril Point, the most westerly promontory of Jamaica. Many cottages are for let along this stretch of road, but most are far removed from the beach. From Negril the road cuts back inland through the villages of Sheffield and Little London, as unlike the originals as it

Sand on Negril Beach

is possible to get, past great houses, some in use some ruined, by the ornamental gates of New Hope (right) and through undulating cane fields and pastures to **Savanna-la-Mar.** This is the principal town of Westmorland, founded in 1703 but subsequently destroyed several times by hurricanes, the last time being in 1912. Little remains of historic interest, but the residue of an old fort exists at the sea end of *Great George Street*, the broad main street, which contains the parish church (on the junction with Murray Street), the courthouse, which has an ornate old cast iron drinking fountain beside it, and the market which offers the usual profusion of local produce. Adjoining the fort is the sugar wharf from which raw brown sugar from three local factories is shipped to refineries abroad. Sugar is tipped from trucks into barges, which carry it out to the ships lying a mile or so offshore. The factory from which most of this sugar comes is **Frome**, the largest sugar factory in Jamaica, 6 miles north of Savanna-la-Mar, and capable of producing 100,000 tons of sugar in a crop lasting from mid-November until June. During this period, it is possible to tour the factory. Cane arrives by rail, cart, and truck to feed the great double series of rollers which grind day and night and exact their tribute from the entire parishes of Hanover and Westmorland. The mills crush out the juice, leaving the fibrous *bagasse*, which is conveyed to the furnaces and burnt to raise the steam which drives every piece of machinery in the factory. Cane juice, initially greenish and murky, is clarified, evaporated, and crystallised to yield the mountain of golden sugar in the bulk store, from which trucks shuttle along to the shipping terminal at Savanna-la-Mar.

Five miles beyond Savanna-la-Mar, on the seaward side of the main A2 coast road, just prior to the junction (Ferris Cross) with the B8 (left) to Montego Bay, is **Paradise Jungle Park**. This recreation area covers 1 000 acres which include jungle, cattle ranch, rivers, tropical farm, bird sanctuary, botanic garden, and a nine-hole golf course. In addition to a restaurant and clubhouse, the park offers facilities for tours, boating, swimming, tennis, golf, archery, horseback riding, or for those who prefer something different, a ride on a two-ton Brahman bull.

The B8 from Ferris to Montego Bay passes by way of Whithorn, Ramble, Montpelier and Anchovy, through scenery, which, although not as ruggedly impressive as the eastern end of the island, is still among the most attractive in Jamaica. The road, which is good quality and quiet, climbs through rolling cattle pastures and cane fields, through villages and little towns and past tiny houses and plots dotted up the hillsides. From Anchovy it descends steeply to the coast, with views of the sea and a distant Montego Bay.

Many inviting side roads lead off the main B8, taking the more enterprising or inquisitive traveller to some of the unspoilt and rarely visited settlements which exist off the not-so-beaten track. For example, from **Whithorn** the side road (right) which climbs 5 miles to **Darliston** offers magnificent views over the coastal plain and the west end of the island, while 3 miles or so after **Ramble** is a side road (left) leading through citrus groves 4 miles to **Lethe**, a quiet village built around a graceful old stone bridge across the Great River. Montego Bay or Savanna-la-Mar are convenient bases from which to explore this interior area more fully.

Area 7   SOUTH COAST

Kingston, Hellshire, Alligator Pond, Treasure Beach
This route follows the coastline wherever possible, and includes an almost complete spectrum of Jamaican landscapes. With the exception of a short unpaved stretch which is bumpy but drivable, the roads are good, and relatively free from traffic. The route crosses Kingston Harbour by the causeway, through the canefields of Bernard Lodge to meet the main road at Spanish Town, leaving it again just after Old Harbour. After crossing the great sugar plain of Vere it meets the coast again at Milk River and follows it through mangrove swamps and near desert, along clifftops and over mountains to the palm lined beaches around Treasure Beach.

From **Half Way Tree**, the route follows the Hagley Park Road across the Spanish Town Road and passes through the charmless harbour development of Newport West. The 1970 vintage Causeway cuts across the western corner of Kingston Harbour, the seventh largest natural harbour in the world, capable of accommodating the biggest liners. It has the additional distinction of being the location of the last recorded shark attack on bathers (1944) in Jamaican waters. The fortress on the promontary to the left of the causeway is **Fort Augusta**, built in 1740 with eighty heavy cannon, to command the shipping channel. It now finds use as a prison, and may be visited by permission of the Superintendent of the General Penitentiary.

At the end of the Causeway we follow a side road to the left through the mangroves to **Port Henderson**, directly across the Harbour from Kingston. This formerly sleepy little fishing village now has a large modern hotel, *Kingston Beach* and is the scene of some fine restoration by the National Trust of the old buildings, including a fishing museum in the *Long House*, and the *Rodney Arms*, a restaurant specialising in reasonably priced seafood.

Behind the buildings looms the bulk of Port Henderson Hill, upon which, reached by a track from the main road, is **Rodney's Lookout**, on a site 716 ft. up with a view of the harbour. After Port Henderson, the road peters out into a rough track which continues past the fortified Apostles Battery, former harbour defence near the sheltered white sand beach of Green Bay. Behind Port Henderson are the **Hellshire Hills**, an arid limestone area containing many cacti and thorn bushes, notable for being one of the few remaining areas of indigenous Jamaican flora and fauna. No attempt has been made to cultivate it and few accidentally introduced species can challenge the already established populations. It is suspected, that the supposedly extinct **Giant Iguana** still exists in the prickly fastness of Hellshire. The area is, surprisingly, being considered for development as a resort. Going back through Port Henderson, the route passes straight through Naggo (corruption of

Negro) Head, and continues through the cane fields of Bernard Lodge Sugar Factory, seen on the left. Shortly after the factory the route meets the main east/west highway, which bypasses Spanish Town at this point. Following the highway left, a side road on the left after 8 miles leads to **Bushy Park**, the largest and best preserved aqueduct in Jamaica. Three miles after Old Harbour (page 87) our route leaves the main road as the B12 at Freetown junction, marked by an Esso petrol station on the left, and runs south through the plain of Vere. Skirting the mangroves along the coastline, which are one of the last refuges for the local crocodiles, the road passes through the sugar terminal of **Salt River**, where sugar from five local factories (Monymusk, New Yarmouth, Sevens, Bernard Lodge, Innswood) is shipped. The sugar is trucked from the huge bulk store on the right of the road across to barges, which transfer it out to ships anchored a mile or so off the coast. Visitors to the quayside are tolerated with good humour and are treated to the fascinating sight of tons of golden sugar cascading down into the barge. Refineries in Britain or North America convert the raw brown sugar into the more familiar refined white variety. One mile after Salt River we take the side road to the left through the cane fields surrounding **Monymusk Sugar Factory**, second largest in the island, and owned by the West Indies Sugar Company, a subsidiary of Tate and Lyle. The factory, which produces all Jamaica's refined sugar, is seen to the right across the cane fields as a tall white chimney.

A small road leads left to Jackson's Bay and to Rocky Point, a scattered little fishing village with an incredibly high population of pigs, goats and stray dogs. Fish and lobsters are available (usually before noon) and a local delicacy worth trying is turtle egg in red wine. Our route carries straight ahead, bypassing Monymusk and Lionel Town, to **The Alley**, which has a well preserved sugar factory windmill (now a library) and an attractive old church, St Peters, dating from 1791. Note the slate roof, an unusual feature in Jamaica, and the quaint old tombstones in the churchyard. In front of the church is one of the largest cotton trees in the island, and other huge specimens are behind the church, in front of the beautiful old wood and stone rectory. Turn right between the large market and a prominent Chinese corner shop, continuing 3 miles through Race Course, to the busy and pleasant little community of Milk River (alias Rest) where a left turn at the T junction leads after a mile to an intersection with a broad road on the right. This is our road to Alligator Pond. The road straight ahead leads to **Milk River Bath**, Jamaica's leading spa, utilising the water from a mineral spring arising at the base of the hill behind the spa. Legend has it that the healing properties of the water were discovered by a runaway slave who, bathing his wounds after a beating, found next day that they had miraculously healed. This legend is shared with Jamaica's other mineral spring, St Thomas, at Bath. Milk River Spring has the highest level of radio-activity of any mineral bath in the world, being three times more powerful than Karlsbad and fifty times higher than Vichy. Rates at this spa are reasonable and it is thus very popular. The river flowing by the door, which gives the area its name, normally resembles coffee more than milk.

The road to **Alligator Pond** starts off with a flourish as a broad modern highway, but relapses for a few miles into a narrow, uneven dirt road. After 4½ miles a small road on the right leads a few hundred yards up (take right fork) to *God's Well*, a very large limestone sink hole 160 ft. deep, containing clear, turquoise water. This area is rocky and arid and is sparsely populated. The Arawaks, however, being predominantly fishermen, managed to settle this stretch of coast and many artifacts and Arawak rock carvings have been found in the area. The local vegetation has hardly changed since they led their simple, idyllic existence there. At Gut River between the forty-nine and fifty-mile posts are pleasant beaches and, by a low stone wall on the left, some deep and beautiful rock pools which are the occasional haunt of alligators. After Gut River the road rises through cactus to the cliff top, which affords views far along the coast to east and west. The shipping installation far to the west is Port Kaiser bauxite terminal. **Alligator Pond** is a quiet fishing village with a great number of bars chiefly patronised by the local fishermen, who land and sell their catches on the beach early each morning. Fishing is still done mainly by pots from the traditional dugout canoes. Turning right in Alligator Pond, the road leaves the coast and climbs into the 2 000 ft. high **Santa Cruz Mountains**, our route taking the first left for Bull Savannah. A digression worth making at this point is a visit to **New Forest Great House**, reached by carrying straight ahead through the next junction (Rowe's Corner) and, after 1¼ miles taking the narrow road on the right up to the house. New Forest, now an elegant ruin, was built in the middle of last century by Charles Fulford, an Englishman who came to Jamaica, married well, and prospered. The house has a series of fine stone arches and a vast hall.

The road to Bull Savannah has views over valleys and coast and turning right at the junction in town, follows the ridges of the Santa Cruz mountains by the appropriately named Bellevue. The scenery en route, valleys, meadows, hamlets, with glimpses of sea and coast, is enchanting.

At Southfield (opposite 19 milepost) 3 miles after Junction, the road on the left leads down to **Lovers Leap**, a 1 500 ft. high escarpment overlooking the sea. From Bellevue the route is straight to Pedro Cross, then left for **Treasure Beach**. The people in this area, among the most helpful and friendly in the country, are noteworthy for another characteristic. After Alligator Pond, complexions become progressively lighter, going from black through brown and *café-au-lait* until, in the Treasure Beach Area, many of the inhabitants have blue eyes and blonde, albeit crinkly, hair. One's immediate thought that these are St Elizabeth Germans is not supported by the lack of German family names in the area. A second popular and equally unsupported explanation is the shipwreck of a Scottish ship in the area, although the fact that skins get lighter as one nears the coast lends some credence to the story. On the coast 2 miles from Treasure Beach village is the terminal point of the trip, the *Treasure Beach Hotel*.

This attractive establishment has ten double rooms, private beach and swimming pool. The telephone has not yet reached this part of the world, so booking is a problem. In season, a cable reservation at least two days in advance is wise. Out of season, except Friday and Saturday, it is reasonably safe to arrive without prior booking. From the hotel it is possible to drive to **Black River** along the coast road, which is rough and uneven, but those who take it are rewarded with some attractive, empty white beaches. The more faint hearted are advised to take the smoother road back to Pedro Cross, bearing left there and driving 4 miles over a partially unpaved road to Watchwell, (look for the telegraph poles going off to the right, and follow them) then via Mountainside and Burnt Savannah to Lacovia on the main Mandeville to Black River road.

Area 8 THE SOUTH WEST

Bluefields, Black River, Bamboo Avenue, Tombstone, Appleton, Accompong, Mandeville.

Including both coast and interior, this route gives an idea of Jamaica's diversity of scenery. It encompasses the superb beaches around Bluefields, the old port of Black River, the Bamboo Avenue, the picturesque Appleton Valley, on the fringe of the Cockpit Country, then through a section of the island's interior, with valleys, meadows and woods, to cool Mandeville. Detours from the main route are trips to the Maroon settlement of Accompong and to Seaford Town, centre of the local 'German' population (ps. 20.67). The area includes such unlikely names as *The District of Look Behind; Me no sen, you no come; Rat-trap; Wait a Bit; Quick Step; and Maggotty.*

ROUTE

Nine miles east of Savanna-la-Mar on the A2 is the fishing village of **Bluefields**, whose white sand beach and clear turquoise water is barely a yard from the road. Formerly the Spanish settlement of *Oristan*, of which no trace remains, a signposted road (left) indicates **Bluefields Great House**, a comfortably old fashioned guest house, where Philip Henry Gosse lived for eighteen months in 1844 whilst collecting material for *A Naturalist's Sojourn in Jamaica*. Bluefields bay was a rallying point for the buccaneer fleets of Mansvelt and Morgan. Five miles east, above the road (left) is Auchindown House, behind which is the ruin of the castle built in 1800 by the member of Clan Campbell who owned both it and nearby Culloden. The A2 follows the coast to Black River which can be bypassed with a saving of 4 miles by taking the side road (left) through Brompton, **Black River** at the mouth of Jamaica's longest river (44 miles) is, with 3 100 population, the main town in St Elizabeth. The approaches to the town contain some quaint old houses with fretwork balconies and shingled roofs, and the road skirts the sea edge as it reaches the town proper at the yellow brick Parish Church of St John (left). Beside the church, the A2 bears left while the main street of town goes straight ahead, following the shore. It contains many old wooden buildings whose upper storey projects out over the footwalk, shielding pedestrians from the sun as they go about their business. The street leads to an iron bridge over the Black River, beside the derelict dock area. A few hundred yards beyond the bridge are beach cottages, rentable by the day, on a fine quiet stretch of shore. Black River boasts one reasonable restaurant, *Sherrif's*, half-way along the main street on the left (upstairs) — speciality is lobster and other sea food, and the town, although neglected, is pleasant. Behind is the **Great Morass**, harbouring a number of crocodiles, ever-diminishing as a result of indiscriminate slaughter by locals and sportsmen. Eight miles north-east of Black River we come to Middle Quarters, a broad junction with the road (left) to Montego Bay via Newmarket. Fifteen miles up this road is, at Struie the junction (right) with a dirt road via Rat Trap to Seaford Town. Middle Quarters is the centre for the sale of cooked shrimps, caught in the Y.S. and Black Rivers, and by stopping your car at the junction you will trigger off a rush of women shrimp vendors. These will press the quality of their shrimps (offered in bowls, large shrimps on top, small underneath) in forceful terms. Beware pepper! Holland Sugar Factory,

Bamboo Avenue

Shrimp Stall, Middle Quarters

across the canefields (right) is the smallest in the island, and was once owned by John Gladstone, father of the British politician. The road follows Bamboo Avenue, the sunlight dappling through an arch of foliage overhead the road. Lacovia, the next township, lines the A2 which is broad and straight at this point, meeting the B6 (left) beside the petrol station at **Tombstone**. A halt at the said petrol station (drinks and patties are on sale) will reveal how the junction got its name, as there, at the roadside before the petrol pumps, are two flat, raised tombstones. One is inscribed to Thomas Jordan Spencer, who died in 1738 at the age of fifteen. The arms are those of Charles Spencer, Earl of Sunderland, who was an ancestor of Sir Winston Spencer Churchill. This road junction offers two routes to Mandeville. The A2, straight ahead, is the shorter of the two, going via Santa Cruz and winding up the escarpment of Spur Tree, with views over the coastal plain, including the giant *Alpart* alumina plant at Nain. The B6 is less busy, longer, and more picturesque, following the Black River inland to the village of **Maggotty**, now site of the latest bauxite operation (Reynolds Jamaica Mines) whose vast complex is immediately north of the town. Our road meets three others in Maggotty, the middle one of which deteriorates as it climbs the 6 miles to the Maroon settlement of **Accompong**, named after a Maroon chief (brother of Cudjoe), and the main Maroon town in this end of the island. Now almost indistinguishable from other Jamaican townships, Accompong comes to life each 6 January, during the celebrations to mark the anniversary of the 1739 treaty which gave the Maroons freedom and autonomy. The main road (right) through Maggotty goes (right) at the bauxite roundabout, then follows and crisscrosses the main railway line (Montego Bay to Kingston) along the **Appleton valley**, one of the loveliest in the island, with level green canefields framed by the surrounding mountains. Soon after crossing the Black River by a narrow rail bridge, the road passes close to *Appleton Sugar Factory and Distillery* (left), the home of Jamaica's most famous and popular rum. After the adjacent village of Siloah the road winds through the canefields to the head of the valley, then climbs up (look back at the view) to Balaclava, a busy one street town, followed by **Oxford** with its nearby (signposted) cave, one of the largest and dryest in the island (see *spelunking*, page 18). Following valleys and hillsides through rolling pastureland and hedge-divided fields, it could almost be Europe, apart from the small towns such as Mile Gully, with the strikingly situated 160-year old St George's Church at the roadside, and Grove Place, the island's largest livestock breeding research centre. At the junction a mile farther on, the road (right) leads 5 miles to Mandeville, while straight ahead carries on via Shooter's Hill to Williamsfield on the main Mandeville to Kingston road. **Mandeville** (pop. 13 000) at 2 000 ft. on a high plateau, is the highest and coolest of Jamaica's main towns, and has long been a favourite residence for expatriate Britons and Americans. It is regarded as the most English town in Jamaica. This impression is given both by the climate and by the town centre, which has a Georgian court house at the edge of a little common, facing a stone, square-towered parish church. The whole effect is of a small English town, even to the oldest golf course in the island, the nine hole *Manchester Club*, being less than half a mile from the town centre. As the bauxite capital of Jamaica, Mandeville is now more American than English, and has a large American population in and around it.

Apart from the town centre, Mandeville is sprawling, formless, and easy to get lost in. The court house (1816) is a handsome building, of stone and wood, its pillared portico set on the steep, balanced sweep of the double staircase. Adjacent to the 1820 church, and its interesting little churchyard, are the large market and the bus station, both of which teem with activity on Saturdays. It is a town not much frequented by tourists, yet, with four modern hotels (*Mandeville, Astra, Dunrobin and Belair*) it is a convenient and pleasant centre from which to visit the central part of the country.

Area 9   THE CENTRE

Old Harbour, Colbeck, May Pen, Chapelton, Christiana, Worthy Park

The main A1 road, passes east to west through Old Harbour and May Pen, skirting the edge of the coastal plain. North of it lie the rugged limestone hills of Jamaica's interior, dotted with picturesque little towns such as Chapelton, Spaldings and Christiana. The route includes Colbeck Castle, the island's great historical enigma, and Halse Hall Great House. The region north of May Pen is rich in relics of former plantation days and includes some fine old ruins. The lovely valley of Lluidas Vale houses Worthy Park, the oldest established sugar factory in Jamaica. The route can be covered on the way to the north or west coasts, but requires a full day to do it justice.

ROUTE

The A2 from Spanish Town takes us to **Old Harbour**, focal point of which is an elaborate iron clock tower in the middle of the junction with the road to Colbeck. Seafood landed at nearby Old Harbour Bay is sold in the town centre, by women higglers whose little stalls line the street corner on the south side of the clock tower. The Colbeck road leads up 2 miles (keep left at the only road junction) to Machado's Tobacco Farm (right) opposite to which a bumpy dirt road leads a few hundred yards up to **Colbeck Castle**. This was until recently the largest building in Jamaica and, at the time of its construction, possibly the largest in the Caribbean. I say 'possibly' because we do not know when it was built, or why, or even by whom. It is usually ascribed to Colonel John Colbeck, who, according to his tombstone in Spanish Town Cathedral, 'came with ye army that conquered this island'. He certainly lived in the area, and as he died in 1682, this would date the castle to 1655 – 1682. If this were so, then it is strange that there is absolutely no mention of the building in any literature or correspondence of that time. Being so vast and situated so close to the main road, it must surely have warranted some comment!

The earliest reference of it comes in the mid-eighteenth century when it appears to have been uninhabited. It is now roofless and floorless and some features suggest that it was, in fact, never completed. For example, the outside walls still contain builders scaffold holes which have never been filled in; the slotted holes in the perimeter wall are too low for firing slits, and were probably drainage holes, as if the wall were intended as a retaining wall for a built-up garden which was never completed. On the other hand, fragments of pottery, tile and glass found by excavating inside the castle suggest that it *was* occupied in quite an elegant manner. It remains a mystery.

May Pen, 12 miles west of Old Harbour, is the fourth largest town in Jamaica and an important commercial centre. We enter it over a narrow iron bridge. The road on the left to Lionel Town passes (5 miles) by Halse Hall great house, now owned and restored by a Bauxite company who allow visitors. May Pen too centres on a clock tower, this one being stone and square and adjacent to a busy market (right). On Fridays and Saturdays May Pen is sheer pandemonium, with people from the countryside swarming in to sell or buy produce. The market cannot contain this colourful, noisy horde and they spill out along the surrounding streets, arguing, inspecting, bargaining or just looking on. Traffic is chaotic. The town itself is uninspiring but is a convenient point from which to tour the hilly hinterland. It is possible to avoid May Pen completely, by taking the right turn beside the Block Factory at Palmer's Cross 2 miles before the town, and driving up the secondary road (1st left) to Moores which has the ruins of a sugar factory after the bridge and the remnants of the Great House crowning the hill above. The fertile lands in this region were among the first to be settled by the English, and the ruins of their plantation works and houses add a mournful undertone to the rugged beauty of this route. A side road 2 miles after Moores leads two miles up to Retreat, whose ruins are much less ruined. The main route continues along the valley to Rock River, where a right turn down a hill, then right again through the river, then left up a private road a few yards, brings us to the ruins of an old plantation works. Artistically built with a fine old aqueduct, and set among citrus groves with a background of mountains, it is an attractive place. Returning to the village we take the straight-ahead centre road to Oaks where we turn left, crossing the Rio Minho at Low Ground and proceeding through citrus groves to **Suttons**. The views are unforgettable — rolling landscape, with random patches of vivid green cane contrasting with darker clumps of trees, set against the distant hills and the far-off mass of Bull Head (2 782 ft.). At Suttons junction we take the right hand road at the signpost (to Chapelton). Just under one mile from the junction, after a little bridge, take the dirt road on the right, which leads a couple of hundred yards to the remnants of **Suttons House** and sugar factory. The Great House, clearly once a fine building, is now dilapidated and inhabited by field workers. The extensive stone and brick shell of the factory lies just beyond, in a clump of trees by the Rio Minho.

Chapelton is a pleasant town whose central park contains the inevitable clock tower which also serves as a war memorial.

After Chapelton comes the junction at **Danks**, where we go east or west.

East (i.e. right) takes us through wild scenery via Arthur's Seat to a T-junction at Crofts Hill, where the left road leads eventually (after 18 miles) to the main north road at Claremont. Two miles along is **Kellits**, in a saddle between two mountains, site of the finest sugar plantation ruins on the route. Taking the right hand road at Crofts Hill then left at Lookout, after half a mile, leads us another 2 miles, down into one of the loveliest of Jamaican valleys, Lluidas Vale, in which is set **Worthy Park** factory, which started making sugar in 1670.

Passing through the valley takes us to Ewarton on the main A1 north/south road.

West at Danks takes us through Savoy (keep left), Pennants and Crooked River to Trout Hall. The road plays tag with the Rio Minho along its valley through citrus groves and pasture. From Trout Hall the right hand road is rough but easily drivable and leads eventually to the north coast by way of **Cave Valley** (scene each Saturday morning of Jamaica's main donkey, horse and mule market, where they are bought, sold, exchanged and even raced), then by Inverness, Alexandria, Culloden, and Brown's Town. It is a fascinating trip.

Carrying straight ahead through Trout Hall we reach Frankfield, another local township, then 10 miles farther, Spaldings, a scattered community attractively sited up and on the hillsides. The village contains Knox College, a progressive junior and high school founded by the Church of Scotland. The town is the centre of one of the island's main ginger growing areas. Two miles after Spaldings (keep right at Clandon after one mile) is the right turn for **Christiana**; on the right is the driveway to *Villa Bella* hotel, a small cosy establishment with eighteen rooms. The climate here is delightful. Christiana is a local metropolis, with over 3 000 inhabitants, and is the centre for small and medium scale local farming. From here it is possible to drive north through Wait-a-Bit to Albert Town, then along the edge of the Cockpit Country to Clark's Town and Falmouth. The road is rough but passable. To the south the road goes via Shooter's Hill and Kendal to Mandeville.

HOTELS

This list of Hotels is reproduced by kind permission of The Jamaica Tourist Board. Prices, which of course are variable, are for the Winter (High) Season 1972/73 in Jamaican $. The accuracy of this information cannot be guaranteed by either the Tourist Board or the publishers. The cost of the Accommodation Tax is not included. (For *key* see page 94.)

Hotels-Kingston and St. Andrew

Hotels	Rooms	Beds	JAMAICAN $ Single	Double	Plan	Key
Abahati+ 7 Grovesnor Terrace, Kingston 8.	28	40	6.00 – 8.00	5.00 – 7.00	EP	a,b,d,e,f,h,s,u.
Beverley Hills+ P.O. Box 208, Kingston 6.	30	60	9.21	7.67	EP	a,b,d,e,k(10%),l,q,r,u.
Casa Monte+ P.O. Box 189, Kingston 8.	17	34	7.67 – 9.97	5.75 – 6.90	EP	a,b,e,f,k(10%),l,n,q,r,u.
Courtleigh Manor+ P.O. Box 601, Kingston 10.	67	110	20.72 – 23.80 14.58 – 17.65 13.04 – 16.11	17.65 – 19.18 11.51 – 13.04 9.97 – 11.51	MAP CP EP	a,b,d(on request),e,f,h, j,l,m,n,o,p,q,r,t,u.
Clieveden Court+ 19 Clieveden Avenue, Kingston 6.	12	24	10.74 8.44	8.44 6.14	MAP CP	a,b,e,l,q,r,u.
Flamingo+ 3 Trevennion Park Rd., Kingston 5.	62	120	16.88 – 17.65 13.04 – 13.80 11.50 – 12.28	14.19 – 15.35 10.36 – 11.50 8.82 – 9.97	MAP CP EP	a,b,e,l,o,q,r,u.
Green Gables+ 6 Cargill Avenue, Kingston 5.	10	17	5.00 – 8.00	5.00 – 7.50	EP	a,c,k(10%),l,u.
Four Seasons 18 Ruthven Road, Kingston 10.	10	20	7.67	5.37	EP	a,b,l.
Indies 5 Holborn Road, Kingston 10.	16	29	6.65 – 8.30	5.80 – 6.65	EP	a,c,e,l,m,q,u.
Liguanea Terrace+ 125 Old Hope Road, Kingston 6.	37	62	11.12 – 13.04	9.97 – 11.50	CP	a,c,d,e,k(10%),l,p,q,r,u.
Mayfair+ P.O. Box 163, Kingston 10.	23	45	6.50 – 10.00	5.00 – 7.50	EP	a,c,d,e,k(10%),l,q,s,u.
Mona P.O. Box 4, Kingston 6.	31	64	17.00	16.00 – 17.00	MAP	a,b,e,j,l,q,r,t,u.
Morgan's Harbour+ Port Royal.	25	50	10.74 – 12.28	8.44 – 9.97	EP	a,b,g,i,k(10%),l,q,r,u.
Mountain Valley Old Stoney Hill Rd., Kingston 8.	10	28	11.00	8.00	CP	a,b,e,q,r,u.
Olympia Residential+ University Crescent, Kingston 6.	19	25	10.74 – 13.80	6.90 – 7.67	CP	a,b,e,k(10%),l,p,q,r,u.
Pegasus+ P.O. Box 333, Kingston 5.	350	700	19.57 – 22.64	12.08 – 13.62	EP	a,b,d,e,g,h,l,m,n,o,p,q,r, t,u.

ALL RATES ABOVE ARE DAILY PER PERSON UNLESS OTHERWISE STATED

+ Member Jamaica Hotel and Tourist Association

Hotels	Rooms	Beds	JAMAICAN $		Plan	Key
			Single	Double		
Roseneath+ 8 Eureka Road, Kingston 5.	22	40	9.97	7.48	CP	a,c,l,q,s,u.
Sheraton-Kingston+ P.O. Box 83, Kingston 5.	400	800	17.65–21.50	11.12–13.04	EP	a,b,d,e,f,h,l,m,n,o,p,q,r,t,u. (FOR MAP ADD US $10.50 PER PERSON DAILY)
Sandhurst+ 70 Sandhurst Crescent, Kingston 6.	40	65	6.14– 7.67	5.75– 7.29	EP	a,c,d,e,g,h,k(10%),l,q,s,u.
Skyline-Kingston+ P.O. Box 70, Kingston 5.	150	269	19.00–22.10	11.88–13.50	EP	a,b,d,e,h,l,o,q,r,t,u.
Sutton Place+ 11 Ruthven Road, Kingston 10.	53	106	9.21	5.75	EP	a,b,d,e,l,r.
Stony Hill Stony Hill P.O.	30	64	19.18 15.35	15.35 10.74	MAP CP	a,b,d,e,(3),h,k,(10%),l,m,n, p,q,r,u.
Terra Nova+ 17 Waterloo Road, Kingston 10.	33	66	16.00	10.00	EP	a,b,e,k(10%),l,n,q,r,u.

Hotels-Ocho Rios and Northshore

Hotels	Rooms	Beds	JAMAICAN $		Plan	Key
			Single	Double		
Carib Ocho Rios+ P.O. Box 78, Ocho Rios.	63	130	32.23–43.74	19.95–25.71	MAP	a,b,d,e,g,i,l,n,o,p,q,r,t,u.
Casa Maria+ P.O. Box 10, Port Maria.	35	70	18.42–24.56	16.88–19.18	MAP	a,c,d,e,f,g,i,k(10%),l,n,o, p,q,s,t,u.
Chela Bay Boscobel P.O.	31	56	10.74–11.51 9.21 7.67	10.74–11.51 9 21 7.67	MAP CP EP	a,b,e,g,i,k(10%),l,o,q,u.
Golden Head Beach+ P.O. Box 1, Oracabessa.	70	140	30.70–33.77	21.50–23.02	MAP	a,b,d,e,f,g,i,l,m,n,o,p,q,r,u.
Hisbiscus Lodge+ Ocho Rios.	17	31	15.35 11.32 9.40	15.35 11.32 9.40	MAP CP EP	a,c,i,q,u.
Jamaica Hilton+ Ocho Rios.	265	530	42.21–53.72	24.94–30.70	MAP	a,b,d,e,g,h,i,k(10%),l,m,n, o,p,q,r,t,u.
Jamaica Inn+ P.O. Box 1, Ocho Rios.	50	100	37.50	31.25–35.40	AP	a,b,e,g,h,i,k(10%),l,n,q,r,t.
Jamaica Playboy Club Hotel+ P.O. Box 63, Ocho Rios.	160	340	30.70–49.88	19.18–28.78	MAP	a,b,d,e,g,i,j,l,m,n,o,p,q,r,t, u.
Little Madness P.O. Box 75, Ocho Rios,	54	116	12.28 9.21 7.67	10.36 6.90 5.75	MAP CP EP	a,b,d,e,i,l,m,r.
Mantalent Inn+ P.O. Box 118, Ocho Rios.	11	22	11.50	8.44	EP	a,c,d,e,i,k,(10%),l,m,o,q,s, u (not under 15 years)
Pineapple Penthouse P.O. Box 282 Ocho Rios.	26	52	15.35 11.50	13.43 9.60	MAP CP	a,b,e,g,h,j,l,m,n,q,r,u.

ALL RATES ABOVE ARE DAILY PER PERSON UNLESS OTHERWISE STATED

+ Member Jamaica Hotel and Tourist Association

Hotels	Rooms	Beds	JAMAICAN $ Single	Double	Plan	Key
Plantation Inn+ P.O. Box 2, Ocho Rios.	65	127	44.50	29.93 – 33.77	AP	a,b,g,h,i,k(12½),l,n,p, q,r,t.
Shaw Park Beach+ P.O. Box 17, Ocho Rios.	116	232	40.67	24.17 – 30.70	MAP	a,b,d,e,g,i,k(10%),l,m,n, o,p,q,r,t,u.
Silver Seas+ Ocho Rios.	56	130	26.09 – 34.53	16.10 – 20.72	MAP	a,b,f,g,h.i,k(10%),l,m,n,o, p,q,r,t,u.
Tower Isle+ Tower Isle P.O.	158	300	23.02 – 53.72	24.94 – 30.70	MAP	a,b,d,(villas),e.f,g,h,i,l,m, n,o,p,q,r,t,u.
Turtle Beach Towers+ P.O. Box 73, Ocho Rios.	503	1006	(23.02 – 69.07 per apartment)		EP	a,b,c,d,e,g,h,i,k(5%),l,u.
Windsor+ St. Ann's Bay.	21	32	10.74	9.60	EP	a,e,h,l,q,u.

Hotels-Discovery Bay-Runaway Bay

Hotels	Rooms	Beds	Single	Double	Plan	Key
Berkeley Beach+ P.O. Box 20, Runaway Bay.	76	160	26.09 – 32.23	17.26 – 20.72	MAP	a,b,d,e,g,h,i,k(10%),l,m,n, o,p,q,r,t,u.
Bubbling Over+ P.O. Box 84, Runaway Bay.	14	28	15.00	11.25	EP	a,b,e,g,h,i,l,q,r,t,u.
Club Caribbean+ P.O. Box 65, Runaway Bay.	60	120	26.09 – 29.16 19.95 – 23.02	19.57 – 23.02 13.43 – 16.88	MAP EP	a,b,e,f,g,h,i,k(10%),l,m, o,p,r,t,u.
Discovery Bay+ P.O. Box 44, Discovery Bay.	24	66	24.56 (Single Suite 3 persons)	46.05 (Double Suite 5 persons)	EP	a,b,d,e.h,i,j,l,o,p,q,r,t,u.
Golf Beach Inn P.O. Box 40, Runaway Bay.	70	140	16.00	11.00	CP	a,b,e,j,l,m,n,o,t,u.
Runaway Bay Hotel+ P.O. Box 58, Runaway Bay.	152	304	49.88 – 56.80	28.78 – 32.23	MAP	a,b,d(on request),e,g,h,i.l, m,n,o,p,q,r,t,u.
Silver Spray Club+ P.O. Box 16, Runaway Bay.	27	54	30.70 – 38.37 23.02 – 30.70	21.10 – 24.94 13.43 – 17.26	MAP EP	a,c,d,e,f,h,j,k(10%),l,q, u(not during Jan. 15-Apr. 15 under 12 years.)

Hotels-Montego Bay

Hotels	Rooms	Beds	Single	Double	Plan	Key
Bay Roc+ P.O. Box 100, Montego Bay.	100	200	41.44 – 44.50	26.09 – 34.53	MAP	a,b,d,e,f,g,h.i,j,k(15%),l,n, o,p,q r,t,u.
Beach View+ P.O. Box 86, Montego Bay.	30	56	8.20 – 10.15	8.20 – 10.15	EP	a,b,g,h,j,l,o,p,q,r,t,u.
Blairgowrie+ P.O. Box 292, Montego Bay.	16	32	23.02 – 26.86	15.35 – 23.02	MAP	a,b,d,e,g,h,i,k(10%),l,q,r,t,u.
Blue Harbour+ P.O. Box 283, Montego Bay.	16	29	8.44	6.14 & 9.60	EP	a,c,e,j,l,q,r,u. (FOR MAP ADD US $8.00 PER PERSON DAILY)
Carlyle Beach+ P.O. Box 412, Montego Bay.	50	100	23.02	13.43 – 14.58	EP	a,b,e,g,i,j,k(10%),l,o,q,r,t,u. (FOR MAP ADD US $9.00 PER PERSON DAILY)
Casa Blanca Montego Bay.	20	37	19.18	11.50	EP	a,b,j,l,m,o,p,q,r,u.

ALL RATES ABOVE ARE DAILY PER PERSON UNLESS OTHERWISE STATED

+ Member Jamaica Hotel and Tourist Association

Hotels	Rooms	Beds	JAMAICAN $ Single	Double	Plan	Key
Casa Montego+ P.O. Box 161, Montego Bay.	98	196	38.37 32.23 30.70	24.56–26.86 18.42–20.72 16.88–19.18	MAP CP EP	a,b,e,j,l,m,n,o,p,q,r,t,u. (Rates quoted are PER ROOM)
Chalet Caribe+ P.O. Box 365, Montego Bay.	28	56	20.72–24.56 13.04–16.88	16.10–19.95 8.44–12.28	MAP EP	a,b,d,e,g,h,i,l,q,r,t,u.
Chatham Beach+ P.O. Box 300 Montego Bay.	115	220	18.42–25.32	13.43–16.10	EP	a,b,e,i,k(10%),l,n,o,q,r,t,u. (FOR MAP ADD US $10.00 PER PERSON DAILY)
The Colony+ P.O. Box 164, Montego Bay.	90	180	46.05–49.88	26.86–28.78	MAP	a,b,e,f,g,h,i,n,q,r,t,u.
Coral Cliff+ P.O. Box 205, Montego Bay.	33	60	15.35	10.74–13.04	EP	a,b,e,g,h,k(10%),l,n,q,r,t,u. (FOR MAP ADD US $8.00 PER PERSON DAILY)
Corniche Villas+ P.O. Box 91, Montego Bay.	46	92	(23.02–26.86 Double Room Apts)		EP	a,c,e,f,j,q,r,t,u.
Doctor's Cave Beach P.O. Box 94, Montego Bay.	65	130	18.42–21.50	13.04–14.58	EP	a,b,d,e,j,k(10%),l,m,n,q,r,t,u. (FOR MAP ADD US $10.00 PER PERSON DAILY)
Fairfield Inn+ P.O. Box 613, Montego Bay.	(NO INFORMATION AVAILABLE AT TIME OF PUBLICATION)					
Fairmont Delisser Drive, Montego Bay.	(NO INFORMATION AVAILABLE AT TIME OF PUBLICATION)					
Good Hope+ Falmouth P.O.	23	40	46.05–53.72	28.78–34.53	AP	a,d,e,g,i,k(15%),l,q,t,u.
Hacton House+ P.O. Box 263, Montego Bay.	27	50	15.35	9.60–11.50	CP	a,b,f,q,r,u(over 12 years)
Half Moon Hotel & Country Club+ P.O. Box 80, Montego Bay.	126	252	66.77–113.60	38.00–61.40	AP	a,b,d,e,f,g,h,i,l,n,o,p,q,r,t,u.
Harmony House+ P.O. Box 55, Montego Bay.	23	42	14.00 9.97	13.23–14.00 9.21– 9.97	MAP CP	a,b,e,g,h,j,l,q,r,u(over 12 years)
Harvey Beach+ P.O. Box 463, Montego Bay.	10	19	11.50	8.44	EP	a,c,g,h,i,k,(10%),l,q,t,u.
Heritage Beach+ P.O. Box 69, Montego Bay.	240	480	18.42–25.32	13.43–16.10	EP	a,b,d,e,g,h,i,k(10%),l,n,o, p,q,r,t,u. (FOR MAP ADD US $10.00 PER PERSON DAILY)
Holiday House P.O. Box 258, Montego Bay.	11	28	(36.84 Double Occupancy)		EP	a,b,d,e,g,h,i,k(10%),q,s,t,u.
Holiday Inn+ P.O. Box 480, Montego Bay.	558	1080	26.09–32.23	18.42–21.50	EP	a,b,d,e,g,h,i,l,m,n,o,p,q,r,t,u. (FOR MAP ADD US $12.50 PER PERSON DAILY)
Island View+ Reading P.O.	25	60	24.56	17.65	MAP	a,b,f,h,j,k(10%),l,n,q,r,t,u.
Malvern+ Montego Bay.	26	52	20.72–22.25 16.88–18.42 15.35–16.88	15.35–16.10 11.50–12.28 9.97–10.74	MAP CP EP	a,b,e,l,q,r,t,u.

ALL RATES ABOVE ARE DAILY PER PERSON UNLESS OTHERWISE STATED

+ Member Jamaica Hotel and Tourist Association

Hotels	Rooms	Beds	JAMAICAN $ Single	JAMAICAN $ Double	Plan	Key
Miranda Hill+ P.O. Box 262, Montego Bay.	40	80	38.37–46.05	23.02–26.86	MAP	a,b,d,e,f,g,h,j,k(10%),l,n,q, r,t,u (over 12 years)
Montego Bay Club+ White Sands P.O.	44	88	15.35–34.53	11.50–21.10	EP	a,b,d,e,j,k(10%),l,o,p,r,u.
Montego Bay Racquet Club+ P.O. Box 245, Montego Bay.	26	55	42.98–46.05	25.32–26.86	MAP	a,b,d,e,f,j,k(10%),l,n,q,r, t,u (Depending on time of year)
Montego Beach+ P.O. Box 144, Montego Bay.	98	192	34.53–42.20	28.78–32.60	MAP	a,b,d,f,g,i,l,n,o,p,q,r,u (Christmas and Easter)
Ocean View P.O. Box 210, Montego Bay.	12	27	14.96 12.66 11.50	10.36–11.90 8.58– 9.60 6.90– 8.44	MAP CP EP	a,b,g,h,j,k(5%),l,q,t,u.
Palm Beach+ P.O. Box 469, Montego Bay.	45	90	21.50–23.02 16.88–18.42 15.35–16.88	18.42–19.18 13.80–14.58 12.28–13.04	MAP CP EP	a,b,e,g,i,l,o,q,r,u.
Hotel Pemco+ 18 East Street Montego Bay.	40	80	21.50 15.35	15.73 9.60	MAP EP	a,b,d,e,j,k(10%),l,n,p,q,r,t,u.
Ramparts Inn+ P.O. Box 34, Montego Bay.	19	38	27.63–30.70 21.50–24.56	18.42–19.18 12.28–13.04	MAP CP	a,b,e,j,k(10%),l,q,s,u.
Richmond Hill Inn+ P.O. Box 362, Montego Bay.	18	34	12.28	11.50	EP	a,c,d,e,f,k(10%),l,n,u.
Ridgely Plaza+ P.O. Box 283, Montego Bay.	19	42	14.20 8.44	12.66 6.90– 9.60	MAP EP	a,b,j,k(10%),l,o,p,q,r,u.
Round Hill+ P.O. Box 64, Montego Bay.	112	224	On request	40.30–53.34	AP	a,b,c,d,e,f,g,h,i,l,n,o,p,q,r, t,u. (not under 3 years)
Royal Caribbean+ P.O. Box 167, Montego Bay.	168	336	42.98–66.77	25.32–37.22	MAP	a,b,d,e,g,h,i,j,l,m,n,o,p,q,r, t.
Royal Court+ P.O. Box 195, Montego Bay.	26	60	17.65	10.74–18.42	EP	a,b,d,e,k(10%),l,m,n (part time),q,r,u.
Sign Great House+ Sign P.O.	24	50	23.02–29.16	13.04–16.10	EP	a,c,d,e,f,g,j,k(10%),l,m,n,q,t,u. (FOR MAP ADD U.S. $10.00 PER PERSON DAILY)
Spanish House P.O. Box 546, Montego Bay.	13	30	13.80	11.50	EP	a,b,e,j,l,q,r,u(over 6 years)
Summit+ P.O. Box 178, Montego Bay.	40	80	12.28–13.80	10.74–11.50	EP	a,b,e,j,k(10%),l,m,o,q,r,u.
Sunset Lodge+ P.O. Box 87, Montego Bay.	40	80	34.53	21.10	MAP	a,b,e,g,h,i,k(10%),l,n,o,p, q,r,t,u.
Toby Inn+ P.O. Box 476, Montego Bay.	24	60	13.80–15.35 7.67– 9.21	11.50–13.04 5.37– 6.90	MAP EP	a,b,e,h,j,k(10%),l,q,r,u.

ALL RATES ABOVE ARE DAILY PER PERSON UNLESS OTHERWISE STATED

+ Member Jamaica Hotel and Tourist Association

Hotels	Rooms	Beds	JAMAICAN $ Single	Double	Plan	Key
Tryall Golf & Beach Club+ Sandy Bay P.O.	55	109	51.42−70.60	30.70−40.30	MAP	a,c,e,f,g,h,i,j,l,n,o,p,q,r,t,u.
Upper Deck+ P.O. Box 16, Montego Bay.	109	218	26.86−29.16	13.43−14.58	EP	a,b,d,e,j,l,o,p,r,u.
Verney House+ P.O. Box 18, Montego Bay.	36	80	15.35−19.18	11.50−13.43	CP	a,c,e,h,j,k(10%),l,p,q,t,u.
Wexford Court Apt.+ P.O. Box 305, Mo. Bay.	18	36	19.18 (Apts.) 15.35 (Rooms)	13.43(Apts.) 9.60 (Rooms)	EP	a,b,d,e,l,r,u.
White Sands Inn+ P.O. Box 284, Montego Bay.	17	34	38.37 32.23 30.70	26.86 20.72 19.18	MAP CP EP	a,b,d,e,j,k(10%),l,q,r.

Hotels-Negril and Southwest Coast

Hotels	Rooms	Beds	Single	Double	Plan	Key
Sundowner+ P.O. Box 5, Negril.	26	52	25.00−28.35	16.67−20.00	MAP	a,b,g,h,i,l,n,u(over 8 yrs.)

Hotels-Port Antonio and East Coast

Hotels	Rooms	Beds	Single	Double	Plan	Key
Bonnie View+ P.O. Box 82, Port Antonio.	24	60	18.00−25.00	14.00−17.50	MAP	a,e,f,s,t,u.
DeMontevin+ 21 Fort George St., Port Antonio.	15	26	12.28	12.28	MAP	a,g,l,q,s,u.
Dragon Bay+ . P.O. Box 176, Port Antonio.	101	202	(49.88−65.23 per cottage)		EP	a,b,d,f,g,h,i,k(15%),l,o, p,q,r,t,u.
Frenchman's Cove+ P.O. Box 101, Port Antonio.	38	76	161.17(House) 115.12(Suite) 90.94(Room)	107.45(House) 76.75(Suite) 60.63(Room	AP	a,b,d,f,g,h,i,m,n,o,p,q,r, t,u, (not in February & March)
Goblin Hill+ San San, Port Antonio.	44	88	23.02−43.17	15.35−28.78	CP	a,b,d,e,f,g,h,i,k(10%),l, q,r,t,u.
Trident Villas & Hotel+ P.O. Box 119, Port Antonio.	16	34	30.70−42.21	26.86−38.37	AP	a,c,d,e,f,g,h,i,l,r,t,u.

Hotels-Mandeville and Southshore

Hotels	Rooms	Beds	Single	Double	Plan	Key
Hotel Astra 62 Ward Avenue, Mandeville.	22	32	14.00 11.50 9.00 8.00	10.00−10.50 8.75− 9.25 7.50− 8.00 7.00− 7.50	AP MAP CP EP	a,d,g,h,k(10%),l,q,r,u.
Belair Caledonia Road, Mandeville.	42	84	17.25−19.50 11.25−13.50	13.50−14.60 7.50− 8.63	MAP EP	a,c,d,e,h,j,k(10%),l,m,n, o,q,s,t,u.
Mandeville Mandeville.	66	132	12.00−13.60 20.00(1 suite)	10.00−12.00 16.00(1 suite)	CP	a,c,d,e,l,q,r,u.
Villa Bella Christiana P.O.	18	38	14.20	14.20	AP	a,h,p,q,t,u.

ALL RATES ABOVE ARE DAILY PER PERSON UNLESS OTHERWISE STATED

+ Member Jamaica Hotel and Tourist Association

Key to be Applied as indicated

AP−American Plan (Three meals) **CP**−Continental Plan (breakfast only) **EP**−European Plan (No Meals) **MAP**−Modified American Plan (Breakfast & Dinner) **(a)**−Private bath/shower **(b)**−Air condo conditioning in all rooms **(c)**−Partial air conditioning **(d)**−Suites (apply for rates) **(e)**−Swimming pool **(f)**−Cottages **(g)**−Fishing, boating etc. **(h)**−Golf available **(i)**−Private beach **(j)**−Beach rights **(k)**−....% added for gratuities **(l)**−Restaurant **(m)**−Night club **(n)**−Orchestra **(o)**−Resort shops **(p)**−Beauty parlour **(q)**−Room service **(r)**−Telephone in all rooms **(s)**−Telephone in some rooms **(t)**−Tennis **(u)**−Children accepted

94

INDEX

Bold type indicates principal references.